ZOO QUEST TO GUYANA

Zoo Quest to
Guyana

by

David Attenborough

ISIS
LARGE PRINT
Oxford, England

Copyright © David Attenborough 1956

First published in Great Britain 1956
by The Lutterworth Press

Published in Large Print 1995 by ISIS Publishing Ltd,
7 Centremead, Osney Mead, Oxford OX2 0ES.
This edition is published by arrangement with
The Lutterworth Press

British Library Cataloguing in Publication Data
Attenborough, David
    Zoo Quest to Guyana. – New ed
    I. Title
    591.9881

ISBN 1-85695-203-7 (hb)
ISBN 1-85695-270-3 (pb)

Printed and bound by Hartnolls Ltd, Bodmin, Cornwall

CONTENTS

CONTENTS

ACKNOWLEDGMENTS

This is the record of three months which four of us spent in British Guyana filming and collecting animals. That our plans were largely fulfilled in this short time was due in no small measure to the help, hospitality and advice that was given us so liberally by everyone we met while we were there, from senior Government officials to Amerindian hunters whose names we never discovered.

To thank them all individually would be impossible but we are especially indebted to Mr. and Mrs. A. F. Mackenzie, Mr. Vincent Roth, Mr. L. D. Cleare and Dr. C. M. Jones who entertained us in Georgetown with great generosity and who gave us invaluable advice in planning the expedition. During our stay on the Rupununi savannahs, Mr. and Mrs. E. Melville, Mr. and Mrs. E. McTurk and Dr. and Mrs. D. Diamond were all unstinting in their help and kindness. Mr. and Mrs. W. Seggar allowed us to monopolize their transport and invade their house while we were in the Mazaruni basin, and Mr. L. E. Dow of New Amsterdam went to a great deal of trouble on our behalf to make our trip on the Canje River a profitable one. We all owe a great deal to Dr. L. Harrison Matthews, Director of the Zoological Society of London who did so much to help us not only in making initial preparations for the expedition, but also in many other ways on our return to this country.

I, personally, am extremely grateful to the British Broadcasting Corporation and particularly to Mr. Leonard Miall, the Head of Television Talks, for sanctioning our plans and making it possible for me to visit Guyana in the first place. I also owe a debt to Dr. Audrey Butt who, after spending a year with the Akawaio tribe, told me much of her unpublished discoveries about the tribe's mythology and customs which has enabled me to understand more clearly some of the things we observed.

Our original intention was that Mr. J. W. Lester should have been co-author of this book, but, tragically, he is still suffering from the illness that overtook him in the later stages of our trip. If he had been able to share in its writing, this account would have greatly benefited from his immense knowledge of tropical wild life.

DAVID ATTENBOROUGH
April, 1956

INTRODUCTION

South America is the home of some of the strangest, some of the loveliest and some of the most horrifying animals in the world. There can be few creatures more improbable than the sloth which spends its life in a permanent state of mute slow motion, hanging upside down in the tall forest trees; few more bizarre than the giant anteater of the savannahs with its absurdly disproportionate anatomy, its tail enlarged into a shaggy banner and its jaws elongated into a curved and toothless tube. On the other hand, beautiful birds are so common as to become almost unremarkable: gaudy macaws flap through the forest, their splendid plumage contrasting incongruously with their harsh maniac cries; and humming birds, like tiny jewels, flit from flower to flower sipping nectar, their iridescent feathers flashing the colours of the rainbow as they fly.

Many of the South American animals inspire the fascination which comes from revulsion. Shoals of cannibal fish infest the rivers waiting to rip the flesh from any animal which tumbles among them, and vampire bats, a legend in Europe but a grim reality in South America, fly out at night from their roosts in the forest to suck blood from cows and men.

For years I had read of all these creatures in the classic accounts written by such naturalists and explorers as Bates, Wallace and Beebe, but I little thought that I should ever be able to visit South America to see them myself. My opportunity to do so came in a roundabout fashion. During my work as a television producer, I was responsible for a series of programmes explaining the meaning of the shape and pattern of animals. To illustrate our points we showed animals from the London Zoo, advised and helped by Jack Lester, the Curator of Reptiles.

After the series was over, he and I held a post-mortem. The programme had been relatively successful, for live animals always provide compulsive television; the attention of viewers is held by the delightful possibility that the creature being shown may bite its handler, escape or behave in some other uninhibited fashion. On the other hand, a tropical animal shown in a studio inevitably seems an oddity, for divorced from its natural surroundings, many of its physical characteristics cease to make sense. It seemed to us that the programmes would have been greatly improved if we had first shown on film an animal in the wild state, and then produced the same creature alive in the studio so that viewers could see it in more detail.

The only way to create such a programme was to organize a joint filming and collecting expedition to the tropics. We proposed such a trip to the authorities in the London Zoo and the B.B.C. and to our delight it was approved. We now had to decide where to go and whom to invite to join us as cameraman.

The choice of place was not difficult. Jack had spent many years collecting animals in Sierra Leone, West Africa. He knew the country well and had a great many personal friends out there who would help us organize our trip. Furthermore, Sierra Leone was the home of an extremely rare bird which had never been exhibited in captivity and which no European had ever seen on its nest. For a long time, it had been Jack's ambition to bring a specimen of this bird back alive to the London Zoo. Unfortunately, its only name was *Picathartes gymnocephalus*, but in spite of the disadvantage of such a tongue-twisting title, we determined to make its filming and capture the main target of the expedition.

The choice of cameraman was more difficult. We needed someone who was experienced in using 16 mm cameras, for we had already decided that 35 mm equipment was too bulky and cumbersome to operate in the difficult country we hoped to reach. He had to have previous experience of expedition work, and also knowledge and interest in animals.

Soon afterwards, I met a short, slight and soft-spoken man of my own age, named Charles Lagus. He had made biological 16 mm films, he had recently returned from a Himalayan expedition in search of the Abominable Snowman, and he also had the useful qualification of having spent some time as a medical student and therefore had a working knowledge of first aid and drugs. I was fully convinced of his affection for animals when I later visited his flat and found it haunted by a giant Himalayan flying squirrel which he had brought back from his last trip and which now squatted on top of the curtain pelmet ready to vol-plane down into the unsuspecting visitor's lap.

I told Charles about our proposed trip and he enthusiastically agreed to join us.

The results of our West African expedition were more successful than we dared hope. We filmed and captured our bird as well as many other creatures, and were able to show them, both alive and on film, in the resulting programmes.

Another expedition was a logical sequel. This time we decided to go to South America. Which area to visit in such a vast and varied continent was a difficult problem, but eventually we selected British Guyana, the only Commonwealth country in the whole of the South American continent. The three of us who had been together in Africa were to go again, and we were to be joined by Tim Vinall, one of the overseers in the London Zoo. His current responsibility was the care of the hoofed animals, but during his long career in the Zoo he had looked after many other types of creature. His was to be the back-breaking and thankless task of remaining at our base at the coast and looking after the animals as we caught them and brought them to him.

So it was that in March 1955, Tim Vinall, Jack Lester, Charles Lagus and I flew to British Guyana.

We landed at the capital, Georgetown, a pleasant city of wide broad streets divided down the centre by lines of scarlet flamboyant trees and delicately-scented frangipani. Elegant modern ferro-concrete buildings stand cheek by jowl with older, white painted, wooden houses, the verandas and porticoes of which are hung with white lacy trellis-work and surrounded by gardens of tropical flowers. The pavements are thronged with people of many nationalities. Owing to Columbus's initial mis-identification, the aboriginal inhabitants of America became known as Indians. The situation in Guyana is complicated by the fact that there are also here many emigrants from India and Pakistan. The Guyanese solve this problem of terminology by contracting "American Indian" to "Amerindian" and referring to the people coming from Bombay and Calcutta as "East Indians". Few Amerindians, however, are to be seen in Georgetown, and the crowds in the city are a *mélange* of African, European, Chinese and East Indian.

After three days of obtaining permits, clearing our cameras and recording apparatus through customs, and buying pots and pans, food and hammocks, we were itching to begin our collecting in the interior. We had already decided on an approximate plan of action. From the map we had seen that most of Guyana is covered by tropical rain forest which extends northwards to the Orinoco and southwards to the Amazon Basin. In the south-west, however, the forest dwindles and gives way to rolling grass-covered savannahs, and lining the coast is a strip of cultivated land where rice fields and sugar plantations alternate with swamps and creeks. if we were to assemble a representative collection of the animals of Guyana, we should have to visit each of these areas, for each harbours creatures which are not to be found elsewhere. We had little idea, however, where we should go in each of the districts and in what order to visit them, until on our third evening we were invited to dinner with three people who could give us expert advice: Bill Seggar, a District Officer in charge of a remote territory in the forests near the far western frontier, Tiny McTurk, a rancher from the Rupununi savannahs, and Cennydd Jones, whose work as doctor to the Amerindians took him to every corner of the colony. We sat up until early in the morning looking at photographs and films, poring over maps and excitedly scribbling notes. When we finally broke up, we had decided upon a detailed campaign, visiting first the savannahs, next the forest, and finally the coastal swamps.

The following morning, we walked into the Airways office to inquire about transport.

"The Rupununi for four, sir?" said the clerk. "Certainly. A plane is leaving to-morrow."

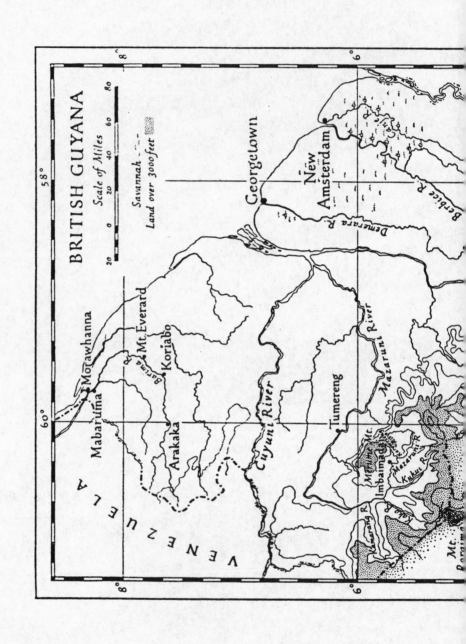

BRITISH GUYANA

Scale of Miles

20   0   20   40   60   80

Savannah
Land over 3000 feet

VENEZUELA

Mabaruma
Morawhanna
Mt. Everard
Koriabo
Arakaka
Barima R.

Tumereng
Cuyuni River
Mazaruni River
Mazaruni R.
Mt. Imbaimadai
Mt. Makarapan
Kukui R.
Kamarang R.
Mt. Roraima

Georgetown
New Amsterdam
Demerara R.
Berbice R.

58°
60°
8°
6°

CHAPTER
ONE

The Savannahs

It was with a sense of great excitement that Jack, Tim, Charles and I clambered into the plane which was to take us south to the savannahs. Nevertheless, we did not expect to find out hearts in our mouths as soon as we did. Our pilot, Colonel Williams, had pioneered bush flying in Guyana and it was largely through his daring and imagination that many of the remoter parts of the colony have become accessible at all. As we took off, however, we discovered that the Colonel's flying technique was very different from that of the pilot who had brought us from London to Georgetown. Our Dakota thundered down the airstrip; the palm trees at the end loomed nearer and nearer, until I thought that something was wrong with the machine and that we were unable to leave the ground. At the very last moment we surged into the air in a steep climb, missing the tops of the palm trees by feet. We all exchanged ashen looks, and after shouting our doubts and worries to one another, I went forward to ask Colonel Williams what had happened.

"In bush flying," he yelled, out of the corner of his mouth, tapping his cigarette into the tin ashtray tacked on to the control panel, "in bush flying, I reckon the most

1

dangerous time is at take-off. If one engine fails then, when you are needing it most, you land with a crash in the forest and there's no one there to help you. I always reckon to get up so much speed on the ground that my momentum is enough to take me up on no engines at all. Why boy, are you-all scared?"

I hastily reassured Colonel Williams that none of us had been in the least bit worried; we were merely interested in the technique of handling aircraft. Colonel Williams grunted, changed the short-focus spectacles that he had worn for the take-off for a long-focus pair, and we settled down for the flight.

Beneath us stretched the forest, a green, velvet blanket spreading as far as we could see in all directions. Slowly it began to rise towards us as we approached a great escarpment. Colonel Williams flew on without altering height until the forest came so close to us that we could see parrots flying above the trees. Then as the escarpment fell, the forest began to change character. Small islands of grassland appeared and soon we were flying over wide open plains veined with silver creeks and freckled with tiny, white termite hills. We lost height, circled over a small cluster of white buildings and shaped up for a landing on the airstrip — a euphemism for a stretch of the savannah which seemed to differ from its surroundings only in that it was clear of termite hills. The Colonel brought the plane down gracefully, and bumpily taxied towards a little knot of people awaiting the plane's arrival. We clambered over the piles of freight lying lashed on the floor of the Dakota and jumped out, blinking in the brilliant sun.

A cheerful, bronzed man in shirt sleeves and sombrero detached himself from the onlookers and came over to meet us. It was Teddy Melville, who was to be our host. He comes from a famous family. His father was one of the first Europeans to settle on the Rupununi and begin ranching the cattle that are now thinly spread throughout the district. He arrived at the turn of the century and took to wife two Wapisiana Indian girls who each presented him with five children. These ten men and women now occupy nearly all the important positions in the district; they are ranchers, store keepers, government rangers and hunters. We soon discovered that, no matter where we went in the northern savannahs, if the man we met was not a Melville, then as like as not he was married to one.

Lethem, where we had landed, consisted of a few white concrete buildings, untidily scattered round two sides of the airstrip. The largest of them, and the only one to have an upper storey, was Teddy's guest-house — a plain rectangular building with a veranda and gaping glass-less windows, which was graced by the title of Lethem Hotel. Half a mile away to the right, on the crest of a low rise, stood the District Commissioner's house, the post office, a store and a small hospital. A dusty red-earth road ran from them to the hotel and continued past a group of ramshackle out-houses into a parched wilderness of termite hills and stunted bushes. Twenty miles beyond, jutting abruptly from the plains rose a line of jagged mountains, reduced by the heat-haze to a smoky-blue silhouette against the dazzling sky.

Everyone for miles around had come to Lethem to meet the plane, for it brought with it long-awaited stores

3

and the regular weekly mail. Plane days therefore are always great social occasions, and the hotel was crowded with ranchers and their wives who had driven in from outlying districts and who remained after the plane had left to exchange news and gossip.

After the evening meal was over, the bare deal tables were cleared from the dining-room and long wooden benches set in their place. Harold, Teddy's son, began setting up a film projector and a screen. Gradually the bar emptied and the benches were filled. Wapisiana cowboys, known as vaqueros, copper-faced with straight lank blue-black hair and bare feet, trooped in and paid at the door. The air was filled with rank tobacco smoke and expectant chatter as the lights were put out.

The entertainment began with some sensibly undated newsreels. These were followed by a Hollywood cowboy film about pioneering the wild west, during which virtuous white Americans convincingly slaughtered great numbers of villainous Red Indians. Hardly tactful one would have thought, but the Wapisiana Indians sat watching their North American cousins being exterminated without any emotion on their impassive brown faces. The story was a little difficult to follow for not only had lengthy sequences been excised during the copy's long life, but it seemed doubtful whether the reels were projected in their correct order, for a tragic and beautiful American girl who was savagely murdered by the Indians in the third reel, reappeared in the fifth to make love to the hero. But the Wapisiana were an accommodating audience, and a pedantic detail of this kind did not spoil their obvious enjoyment of the

4

big-fight scenes, which provoked rounds of enthusiastic applause. I suggested to Harold Melville that the film was perhaps an odd choice, but he assured me that cowboy films were by far the most popular type of any they showed. Certainly one could believe that sophisticated Hollywood bedroom comedies would seem even greater nonsense to the Wapisiana.

After the show, we went upstairs to our room. In it were two beds equipped with mosquito nets. Two of us obviously had to sleep in hammocks, and Charles and I claimed the privilege. It was an opportunity which both of us had been thirsting to seize ever since we had bought our hammocks in Georgetown. We slung them from hooks fastened in the walls, with a highly professional air. The results however, as we realized after a few weeks of experience, were hopelessly amateur. We had hitched them far too high and had tied them with enormously elaborate knots that were going to take a considerable time to loosen in the morning. Jack and Tim stolidly climbed into their beds.

The next morning there was little doubt as to which pair of us had spent the more comfortable night. Charles and I both swore that we had slept like logs and that sleeping in hammocks was second nature to us. But it was hardly true, for neither of us had then learnt the simple technique of lying diagonally across the stretcherless South American hammock. I had spent most of the night trying to lie along the length of it, with the result that my feet were higher than my head and my body was slumped in a great curve. I had been unable to turn without breaking my back, and I got

5

up that morning feeling that I should be afflicted with permanent curvature of the spine.

After breakfast, Teddy Melville came in with the news that a large party of Indians had started fishing in a nearby lake by the traditional method of poisoning its waters. There was a chance that in the process they would come across other animals which might be of interest to us, and Teddy suggested we should ride over to have a look. We got into his truck and set off across the savannahs. There was little to prevent us from driving wherever we wished. Here and there were tortuously weaving creeks, but they were easily avoided; we could see them from a considerable distance away, their banks being fringed by bushes and palm trees. Otherwise the only obstacles in our way were clumps of stunted sandpaper bushes and termite hills — tall, crazily-spired towers, sometimes standing singly and sometimes concentrated in groups so dense that at times it seemed we were driving through a giant graveyard. A few well beaten tracks across the savannahs link one ranch to the next, but the lake we were to visit was isolated and before long Teddy branched off the main trail and began threading bumpily between the bushes and the termite hills, following no track but simply relying on his sense of direction. Soon we saw a belt of trees on the horizon marking the site of the lake we were to visit.

When we arrived, we found that a long arm of the lake had been dammed with a barricade of stakes. Into it the Indians had crushed special lianas which they had gathered many miles away in the Kanuku mountains. All around were fishermen with bows and arrows at the ready, waiting for the fish to become stupefied by the poisonous sap of the lianas and float to the surface. Indians clung to branches of trees overhanging the lake's margin; they perched on specially built platforms in the middle of the water; some stood on small improvised rafts and others patrolled up and down in dug-out canoes. In a clearing on the bank the women had lit fires and slung hammocks and now sat waiting to clean and cure the fish as soon as the men brought them in; but nothing so far had been caught and the women were getting impatient. Their menfolk had been foolish, they said scornfully: too big a section of the lake had been dammed and too few lianas had been gathered in the forest, so that the poison was too weak to affect the fish. Three days of hard work in damming and platform building had been wasted. Teddy talked to them in Wapisiana and gathered all this information as well as the news that one of the women had seen a hole in the bank on the other side of the lake, which she said was occupied by a large animal. What kind of animal it was, she was not sure; it might be either an anaconda or a caiman.

The caiman belongs to the same group of reptiles as the crocodile and alligator, and to the layman all three animals look very much alike. To Jack, however, they are very different, and though all three are found in the Americas, they each have distinctive habitats. Here on the Rupununi, Jack said, we could expect to find the black caiman, the largest species in its own group, which is reputed to grow up to twenty feet long. Jack admitted that he would rather like a "nice big caiman" and, come to that, he would also be quite glad to catch a sizeable anaconda. As the animal in the hole might turn out to be one or the other, he felt we really should try to catch it. We all climbed into dug-out canoes and paddled across the lake with one of the women to guide us.

On investigation, we found that there were two holes — a small one and a large one, and that they were connected with each other, for a stick pushed down the smaller one provoked splashes from the other. We barricaded the smaller hole with stakes. To prevent the unknown creature from escaping through the larger one and, at the same time, to allow it enough space to emerge and be caught, we cut saplings from the bank and drove them deep into the mud of the lake bottom in a semicircular palisade around the entrance. We had not yet seen our quarry and no amount of prodding through the smaller hole would drive it out, so we decided to enlarge the big hole by cutting through the turfy bank. Slowly we hacked away the roof of the tunnel, and as we did so the bank shook with a subterranean bellow that could hardly have been produced by a snake.

Cautiously peering through the stakes of the palisade into a gloomy tunnel, I just distinguished, half submerged in the muddy water, a large yellow canine tooth. We had cornered a caiman, and judging from the size of the tooth, a very large one.

A caiman has two offensive weapons. First and obviously, its enormous jaws; and second, its immensely powerful tail. With either it can inflict very serious injuries, but fortunately the one we were tackling was so placed in its hole that we only had to pay attention to one end at a time. Having had that momentary glimpse of its teeth, I knew which end was uppermost in my mind. Jack was paddling about in the muddy water inside the stakes trying to work out how the caiman was lying and how best to tackle the job of catching it. It seemed to me that if the beast elected to come out in a hurry, Jack would have to jump very quickly to avoid losing a leg. For my part, I felt I was quite near enough to danger wading thigh-deep farther out in the lake, manoeuvring Charles in a canoe at a sufficient distance to get good film shots of the proceedings. In the event of the caiman making a lunge at Jack, I was quite sure that it would come with such a rush that it would knock our flimsy palisade flat, and whereas Jack could leap for the bank, I should have to wade several yards before I reached safety. I was in no doubt that the caiman, in such a depth of water, would be able to move faster than me. For some reason or other — perhaps my nervousness showed itself more than I imagined — I seemed unable to keep the canoe steady enough to make it practicable for Charles to work, and after I had given it a particularly violent lurch, which nearly threw him and his camera into the water, he decided that his apparatus would stand less chance of getting wet if he joined me wading in the lake.

Meanwhile, Teddy had borrowed a raw-hide lasso from one of the Indians, and he and Jack, kneeling on the bank, were dangling it in front of the caiman's nose in the hope that it might lunge forward towards Charles and me and, in doing so, thrust its head through the noose. It roared and thrashed the sides of its tunnel so violently that the whole bank quivered, but very sensibly it refused to come out any further. Jack cut more of the bank away.

By now there were some twenty Indians watching the proceedings and offering suggestions. To them it seemed incomprehensible that we should wish to catch the creature alive and unharmed. They were in favour of despatching it there and then with their knives.

At last, with the aid of two forked sticks to hold the noose wide open, Jack and Teddy coaxed the lasso round the caiman's ugly black snout. This plainly infuriated the beast and with a twist and a roar it shook the noose off. Three times the rope was on and three times it was shaken off. It went round a fourth time. Slowly, with the sticks, Jack eased it up towards the caiman's head. Then suddenly, before the reptile realized what was happening, he drew the noose tight and the dangerous jaws were secured.

Now we had to guard against a blow from its huge tail. The situation began to look more alarming from where Charles and I were standing, for, having tied another noose round the caiman's jaws for safety, Teddy told the Indians to uproot the palisade. There was nothing now but open water between Charles and me and the caiman which lay with its long evil head projecting out of the hole, glaring at us malevolently with yellow unblinking eyes. Jack, however, jumped down from the bank into the water immediately in front of the hole, taking with him a long pole he had cut from a sapling. Bending down, he pushed the pole into the tunnel so that it lay along the reptile's scaly back, and reaching inside he secured it by tying a half-hitch round the pole and under the animal's clammy armpits. Teddy joined him and, inch by inch, they drew the brute out of its hole, tying half-hitches around its body and on to the sapling as it emerged. The back legs, the base of the tail, and finally the tail itself were securely tied and the animal lay safely trussed at our feet, the muddy water lapping round its jaws. It was just ten feet long.

It now had to be ferried across the lake to the trucks. We hitched the front end of the pole to the stern of a dug-out canoe, and towing the caiman behind us we paddled back to the women's encampment.

Jack supervised the Indians as they helped us to load the caiman on to the truck and then he methodically inspected its bonds one by one to see that none was chafing. The women, having no fish to cure, gathered round the truck, examining our capture and trying to decide why on earth anybody should value such a dangerous pest.

We drove off back across the savannahs. Charles and I sat on each side of the caiman with our feet within six inches of its jaws, trusting that the raw-hide lassoes were as strong as they were reputed to be. We were both jubilant at having caught such an impressive creature so early. Jack was less demonstrative.

"Not bad," he said, "for a start."

CHAPTER
TWO

Anacondas and Ant-Bears

The anaconda is reputed to be the biggest snake in the world. Travellers have reported seeing monstrous examples over eighty feet long, but the longest actual skin on record is something over thirty feet and that may well have stretched a little after removal from its owner. Naturally Jack wanted one for his Reptile House in the Zoo and we asked Teddy if they were common in Lethem.

"Yes," he said, "there are plenty of them in the creeks around here. We call them water camoodie. They take quite a few of my young calves, and there was one woman down in the southern savannahs whose child was nearly killed by one. She came out of her hut just after the snake had first laid hold of her little daughter, and she was able to shoot it before the child was crushed to death. Of course," he continued, looking quizzically at Jack, "I'm not sure how you are going to catch one. You could set traps, I suppose, but I guess you might have to wait months before you caught anything. On the other hand you might be lucky enough to spot one resting on the bank of a creek, and then you could try jumping on it and tying it up before it's got time to slip back into the water. How about that?"

Jack nodded. "Scragging," he said cheerfully, "is the only method I know that is any good. If it's a big one, of course, a single man could not cope with it by himself; all of us would have to leap at the same time. I suppose you, Charles, will be busy with your camera if we do see one." He looked at me with confidence. "But you are game, aren't you?"

I cleared my throat a little nervously, but before I could say anything Teddy broke in.

"Come to think of it," he said, "there was an American going around some time ago offering a big reward for a camoodie over twenty feet long, and I did hear that someone over the river in Brazil had caught one which he reckoned would get him the money. Why not go over and see if the snake's still there?"

"Is it far away?" I asked anxiously, fearful lest this stroke of luck should strike Jack as being impracticable.

"No, no," said Teddy, "about a couple of hours' run in a jeep to the Ireng River at Pirara. This Brazilian keeps a store on the other side, but perhaps it's only a rumour and if he had got a camoodie he's probably sold it by now."

But I was all for finding out and Jack agreed, so that afternoon we drove off again through the savannahs towards the Ireng river. Jack and a guide were in one jeep and Charles and I followed behind. Within a few minutes we were so begrimed and choked by the dustcloud in Jack's wake that Charles and I trailed a quarter of a mile behind him to allow the dust to settle before we sent it flying again.

One hour's drive brought us to Pirara, Ben Harte's ranch. Ben is married to one of Teddy Melville's sisters and living with them is his mother-in-law, Mamai Maria, one of the two Indians whom the original Melville had married when he first came into the country. She is now a very old lady, though neither she nor anyone else was exactly certain how old she is. Teddy thought that she was something over eighty. We looked forward very much to meeting her, but when Ben came out to greet us he told us that we were unlucky.

"She's gone out," he said. I asked where she had gone, wondering where it was that an old lady of over eighty *could* go to in this wild country.

"Well, boys," answered Ben, "I reckon she must have gone up-river fishing."

We looked surprised, but Ben evidently saw nothing in the least unusual in what he said. We changed the subject.

"Have you heard about a water camoodie over in Brazil?"

Ben tipped his sombrero over his eyes and scratched his grizzled head.

"Did hear some talk about that. They might have one. My son Elmo will take you over; he knows 'em there. But ain't you hot? Come in for a little bit of rum."

We went inside Ben's house and sat down to an iced rum and ginger.

Within a few minutes Elmo arrived, and after a final

drink we left the house, and with Elmo as our guide drove to the belt of trees which fringed the river. Having parked, we followed Elmo along a little track through the trees and down to the banks of the Ireng — a wide, turbulent, muddy river, superficially placid, but blistered with circular rippling eddies which betrayed its deceptive force and speed. Elmo put his fingers into his mouth and gave a piercing whistle.

A quarter of a mile downstream, we could see two tiny canoes moored at a landing and signs of cultivation on the banks above. Elmo whistled again. A small white figure appeared on the bank, waved its arms and then disappeared. We sat down and waited. Elmo watched us smacking ourselves in a vain endeavour to kill the kaboura flies that were pestering us, each of their bites drawing a little drop of blood and itching maddeningly.

"Don't do no good to knock yourselves about like that," he observed to no one in particular, "they'll go on biting anyway, so you might just as well let 'em and save your energy."

By this time the tiny figure had reappeared, descended the bank and got into one of the canoes. Elmo told us that this was the storekeeper. Very slowly, paddling furiously against the stream, he worked his way up the farther bank. He drew level with us, passed us, and then turned his bows into the main stream, paddling even harder to get across. By the time he was over, the current had swept him down to where we were standing.

When he disembarked Elmo asked him in Portuguese if he still had the snake. To our delight he had. As we swept down river in his fragile canoe, I was optimistically trying to devise some way in which we could transport half a ton of snake across such a river back to the jeeps.

We landed, climbed up rough, mud steps in the bank, and followed the Brazilian back to his store. A fragile and charming raven-haired woman came out to greet us. She smiled and we shook hands, but she said nothing. Her husband gestured to a large outhouse, and led us over to it.

Two-thirds of the interior was occupied by a stockade of posts driven deep into the mud floor and covered by other posts lashed securely to one another to form a roof. The Brazilian cautiously flashed a torch through a chink between the posts and then gently lifted two loose ones out of their holes so that we might see inside. The hut was windowless and so dark that it was difficult to distinguish anything. Then we saw a great shining flank as thick as a telegraph post and suddenly realized that half of the floor was covered by the black, sprawling coils of a snake.

We played the torch over it. In the centre of the dark tangle a wedge-shaped, blunt-nosed head rested on one of the coils, and two unblinking, beady eyes glinted in the light of our torch. Jack seemed unimpressed.

"He looks quite big and in fairly good condition," he said, cautious lest any sign of enthusiasm should increase the price. "How did he manage to catch him?"

Elmo repeated the question in Portuguese to the storekeeper.

"He didn't catch him at all," Elmo translated. "He says his wife did. She was out on the savannahs in a horse and cart and saw this brute in a drying lake, so she lassoed its head, hauled it on board the cart and tied it up."

The posts were replaced and firmly bound in position. We walked back into the store. The fragile huntress was awaiting us with drinks of cashew juice liqueur. She smiled to us all again and said nothing.

Meanwhile, her husband bargained for the snake she had caught. Teddy had been quite right in thinking that a reward had been offered by an American. The storekeeper maintained that his anaconda was over twenty-seven feet long and said that he could get at least a thousand dollars for it if he took it down to Boa Vista on his next trip. We did some rapid calculations. A thousand dollars was over two hundred pounds. We could not be certain of getting the reptile back to London in good condition and even if we did it might not survive long, for large anacondas are notoriously reluctant feeders in captivity. Jack explained that it might be possible to force food down its throat, but that snakes rarely live long under such treatment. It depressed me to think that we might have to return empty-handed when such a magnificent monster lay captive only a few yards away, but Jack decided that the highest bid he could make was one hundred and fifty dollars. The Brazilian laughed good-naturedly. He was confident that a thousand dollars was his, as soon as he took the anaconda to Boa Vista. We could not possibly raise enough money to compete with such an offer and so, with final drinks to show that we both regretted our inability to help one another, we parted and walked back to the river.

We drove Elmo back to Pirara. As we entered the courtyard, a small slim woman walked slowly out of the house. It was Mamai Maria, returned from her fishing. She wore a bright, flowered cotton frock and her long hair, once jet black but now silver grey, hung down to her shoulders. Elmo introduced us in Portuguese and we shook hands.

"Did you have good luck fishing?" I asked.

She smiled gently and nodded.

"I'm afraid she doesn't understand English," Elmo explained, "but she is very fond of an English cigarette, if you have any."

Charles produced a packet. Mamai lit one, took long slow puffs and stared vacantly into the distance, screwing up her eyes against the violent sun. Looking at her tranquil wrinkled face, it was hard to believe that she had lived through tempestuous pioneering days on the savannahs. I longed to ask her about them, but Mamai smiled again, turned and shuffled back to the house.

We returned to Lethem profoundly depressed at our failure to secure the anaconda, and after discussing the situation that evening with Teddy over glasses of rum, we decided there was only one thing for it — we should have to scrag one after all.

"One of my vaqueros," said Teddy, "reckons he saw a water camoodie in a swamp on the outskirts of the ranch. If you'd like to try scragging that, we could go out there to-morrow and have a look."

Early next morning we loaded cameras and food, ropes and sacks into a truck and drove off south through the savannahs to a tiny out-station on Teddy's ranch — a small, wooden house surrounded by a grove of cashew trees. They were laden with ripening fruits, like small, yellowing pimentos, beneath each of which hung a naked curling nut. Piles of the fruit lay rotting on the ground. We tasted some, but though they were sweet their juice was harsh and left us with rough mouths. We decided that we preferred them when they had been crushed and the juice distilled into the cashew liqueur which we had tasted over the Ireng river in Brazil.

While we were sampling the cashews, Teddy had recruited the two vaqueros who lived in the huts, one of whom had seen the anaconda a few days before, and together we walked down towards the swamp where the snake was supposed to live. On our way we saw the skeleton of a tree on the top of which had been built an ants' nest, which looked like a brown earthen football. As we passed, a parrot flew out from a hole in the side. It was likely that she had built her own nest inside that of the ants and I shinned up to look. I peered in but though I could see nothing, I heard a faint chirping. Gingerly, I put my hand inside and brought out a naked little chick. As with a human baby, its head seemed too large for its body and its enormous beak, which would later be a useful nut-cracker, now appeared to be only an absurdly comic roman nose. Cradled in my hand, it goggled at me and then sat back and begged for food. It was so charming that I longed to keep it to try and rear it by hand, but I knew that it was so young that I had little chance of being successful, so, regretfully, I gently put the little creature back in its nest.

Meanwhile, Teddy had found something in the fringes

of the swamp. He pointed to a pug-mark in the mud. "Ant-bear," he said laconically.

We knelt down and examined it and were able to pick out the marks left by the enormous claws with which the ant-bear's feet are armed. Its forelegs are immensely muscular and with them it can rip apart concrete-hard termite hills in search of the soft larvae which are its main food. Normally the ant-bear is a harmless creature, but though it has no teeth it is a dangerous animal to provoke, for its forelegs and claws are lethal offensive and defensive weapons. If it can manage to embrace its opponent with its forelegs, the unfortunate victim has little chance of escaping or of surviving the terrible wounds inflicted by the vicious claws. Teddy told us that he had lost several of his dogs that way. Once he had managed to rescue one from the clutches of an ant-bear, but the wounds in its back were so deep and severe that the dog lived only a few hours.

As Teddy was telling us this, I recalled seeing a picture in an old edition of Waterton's *Wanderings in South America*, which vividly illustrated an ant-bear thrown on its back and grappling with a jaguar, which plainly was not going to survive long.

But we were looking for anacondas, and, leaving the ant-bear spoor, we rose to our feet and walked towards a little thicket of bushes and tall grass that was flourishing in the swampy hollow. It was there that the snake had been seen. We could see no sign of it, but in any case we could hardly expect to spot it from several yards away. Charles stopped behind and set up his cameras for what he expected, and I feared, might turn out to be a scragging match of the most dramatic kind. Teddy, Jack and I walked slowly and cautiously into the thicket, but we still could not see any sign of the snake.

And then, suddenly, as we were poking in the undergrowth there was a rustle, and a few yards in front of us a great shaggy form shambled to its feet and set off at a gallop through the hollow and out into the savannahs on the other side. It was the ant-bear! Jack and Teddy immediately gave chase, while I shot out of the thicket, yelling to Charles to bring his camera round to the other side. Perhaps my shouts were not very explicit. Charles at any rate was unable to interpret them and stood there, arms akimbo, dumbfounded and slightly irritated at being interrupted in the middle of his technical photographic calculations.

Within seconds the ant-bear came into sight, hotly pursued by Jack and Teddy, and Charles whipped into action. The ant-bear had got a considerable lead on its pursuers, who by now were flagging in the baking sun. But they had managed to make the animal veer round towards me. I took over the chase from them and, starting fresh, I slowly overhauled it. Running as fast as I could and stumbling over roots and tussocks, I found myself wondering what I would do if I caught up with the creature. I had almost done so when Jack, who was standing puffing a hundred yards away, shouted out, "Grab hold of its tail!"

Without thinking, I did as I was told. The great creature, goaded into fury, lurched round, reared up slightly on its hind legs and took a swing at me with one of its forelegs. Waterton's picture flashed through

21

my mind and I was so startled that I fell backwards. By the time I had recovered the ant-bear was once more galloping across the savannahs with its tail waving behind it like a banner.

My bravery, or foolishness, had not been entirely wasted however, for it had checked the animal long enough for one of Teddy's vaqueros to catch up with it. He whirled his raw-hide lasso round his head and cast it neatly and precisely around the ant-bear's neck, bringing the beast to a growling halt. Within seconds, the rest of us had caught up with it. Teddy ran back and fetched the truck on to which we gently loaded our capture.

The ant-bear, or to give it its more usual name the giant anteater, is one of the world's most curious creatures. It grows up to a length of six feet and is covered with shaggy, dirty-grey hair. It uses its bushy, flag-like tail as a blanket with which to protect itself from the rain and the sun when it is lying up during the day. Its toothless jaws are elongated into a tube two feet long, ending in a tiny mouth, and it eats by flicking out its long thong-like tongue, covered with sticky mucus, which gathers up the ant and termite larvae on which it lives.

Now that they were securely tied, we examined its great forelegs which could have been so dangerous to us. Its claws were fully four inches long and quite obviously prevented the animal from walking in the normal way. It does, in fact, fold its claws back, so keeping them sharp, and walks on its knuckles, which are bare of hair and covered in hard skin.

The capture of the ant-bear had caused such a

commotion that we could hardly expect to find our anaconda dozing in the sun on the bank in the swamp. We turned back, however, on the off chance that it might be still there. There was no sign of it, and indeed though we were on the look-out throughout our stay on the savannahs, we never caught a glimpse of an anaconda apart from the one which we had failed to buy in Brazil.

CHAPTER
THREE

Karanambo

After a week on the savannahs we found, rather to our surprise, that we had assembled quite a large menagerie. Teddy Melville had contributed by giving us several of the pets that roamed about his house — Robert, a raucous macaw, two trumpeter birds which had been living semi-domesticated lives among the chickens, and Chiquita, his capuchin monkey, who, though very tame, had the trying habit of slyly stealing things from our pockets when we were innocently playing with her.

The Indian vaqueros also knew of our wants and had brought us many kinds of animals. The most extraordinary of their captures was a mata-mata turtle, which an Indian had found while he was fishing. I doubt if we would ever have noticed it, for its camouflage was almost perfect. Its rough irregular shell was exactly the same colour as the leaves that often carpet the bottom of the pools in which it lives, and its flattened spade-like head was so extensively disguised that it was hardly recognizable at all. All along its neck and beneath its chin hung ragged tatters of skin resembling twigs and leaves, which effectively broke up the tell-tale outline of its head and neck. It has even been said that the mata-mata is able to wave these appendages and use them as lures to entice unsuspecting creatures close to the enormous mouth that spreads round the flattened head in a great bland grin. Its nostrils were placed on the top of a thin projection, so that when the turtle lay submerged in a pool, this grotesque twig of a nose just broke the surface of the water and enabled the creature to breathe.

The problem of housing all these animals became increasingly difficult. At first we were able to convert beer crates into comfortable cages by the simple method of adding specially-made wire fronts which we had brought with us. But the supply of crates, even in such a thirsty country as the Rupununi, was soon exhausted, and anyway we had many animals for which beer crates were not suitable.

Fortunately, early in our stay we came across Bolotov, a tall, spare man with a deeply lined grey face. He had been a prisoner on Devil's Island, the French penal settlement off the coast of Cayenne, and after serving his sentence he had migrated north to the savannahs to earn his living as a carpenter. We met him on our second day in Lethem, when Jack, Tim and I were staring at our single roll of wire netting, wondering how on earth we were going to convert it into cages for the caiman and the ant-bear. Bolotov stood by us for a few minutes without speaking and then, with a very marked Central European accent, he said softly, "Please, if you wish it, maybe I am able to help you." We turned to him with gratitude and suggested that he might start by devising something to house the caiman. Cautiously he measured the reptile

25

as it lay, tied to its pole. Then he disappeared into his workshop, and within a few hours he had constructed a stout wooden crate, tailor-made to fit the brute.

The task of tending the creatures fell to Tim Vinall. Each morning he threw buckets of water over the caiman as it lay in its cage, so that its hide remained moist and did not become parched and cracked. The giant anteater spent most of its time curled up in one of Bolotov's most capacious cages, asleep beneath its tail. At first it worried us by refusing to feed, but on the second day, to our relief, it began investigating the sections of termite hill that Tim had dumped in one corner, and soon we were fascinated to watch its tongue whipping out and extracting the white larvae from their earthen cells. Although this was heartening, the problem of the animal's diet was by no means solved, for we could not provide termites on the long voyage home and there would be none for it when it arrived in the London Zoo. After a few days, therefore, Tim began offering it a substitute food of minced meat, raw eggs and condensed milk, sprinkled with termite larvae. He also added some earth, for in its wild state the anteater inevitably swallows much of the matrix of the termite hills, and this roughage may be necessary for proper digestion. Gradually Tim reduced the amount of larvae in the mixture, and the anteater finally became so fond of its new food that if Tim was careless enough to leave a prepared dishful within eighteen inches of its cage, it would stick its nose close to the bars, flick its tongue across the intervening distance and lick up half the contents of the dish before Tim was aware of what was happening.

26

Teddy was not surprised that our anteater was settling down so well, for several people on the savannahs had kept them as pets. He told us of one rancher who had been badly troubled by termites. They had invaded his house and eaten away the floor boards and the wall posts. A government adviser on pest control, visiting the savannahs, called on him and heard all about his trouble. He prescribed a new chemical insecticide, but the rancher had already tried it. He then suggested another, but that too had failed. "Well, all I can recommend," said the adviser ironically, "is that you keep an ant-bear."

"Just look in here," said the rancher pointing to the back of the room, where a young ant-bear was lying curled up asleep in a tiny specially-made hammock. The expert had nothing further to suggest.

With our large collection of animals well established in Tim's care, we decided to extend our search beyond the immediate neighbourhood of Lethem, and to visit Karanambo, sixty miles away to the north. Karanambo is the home of Tiny McTurk, who had invited us to stay with him when we met on our third day in Georgetown. We said good-bye to Tim, climbed into a borrowed jeep, and set off.

After three hours' driving through the scrubby featureless savannahs, we saw on the horizon a belt of trees lying across the line of the trail we were following. There was no sign of a gap or clearing to suggest there was a way through and it looked as if the track must dwindle and peter out. We were sure that we had lost our way, but then we saw that the path plunged straight into the trees, down a narrow gloomy tunnel just wide enough to admit our jeep. The tree-trunks on either side were interwoven with small bushes and lianas, and branches met overhead to form an almost solid ceiling.

Unexpectedly, sunshine flooded down on us. The belt of bush ended as suddenly as it had begun and in front of us was Karanambo; a group of mud brick and thatched houses, sprinkled around a wide, gravelled clearing and interspersed with groves of mangoes, cashews, guavas and lime trees.

Tiny and Connie McTurk had heard the jeep and had come out to greet us. Tiny was tall and fair and dressed in an oily khaki drill shirt and trousers, for we had interrupted him in his workshop where he was fashioning new iron arrowheads. Connie, shorter, slim and neat in blue jean trousers and a blouse, greeted us warmly and showed us into the house. We then entered one of the most curious rooms I have ever visited. It seemed to contain a world of its own, the old and primitive, and the new and mechanical — a microcosm of life in this part of the world.

Room, perhaps, is not an entirely accurate word, for on two adjoining sides it was open to the sky, the bounding walls being only two feet high. Straddling the top of one of them was a leather saddle, and just outside a long wooden rail carried four outboard engines. Behind the wooden walls on the other two sides of the room lay the bedrooms. A table against one of these walls was covered with radio apparatus, with which Tiny maintained contact with Georgetown and the coast, and by the side of it stood a large set of shelves crammed with books. On the other wall hung a large clock and a barbaric assortment of guns, crossbows, longbows, arrows, blowpipes, fishing lines and an Indian feather headdress. In the corner, we noticed a stack of paddles and an Indian earthenware jar full of cool water. In the place of chairs there were three large gaily-coloured Brazilian hammocks slung across the corners of the room, and in the centre, its feet embedded deep in the hard-packed mud floor, stood a giant table about three yards long. Above us, on one of the beams, hung a line of orange-coloured maize heads, and, here and there, stretching across the beams, a few planks provided a spasmodic semblance of a ceiling. We looked around admiringly.

"Not a nail in the place," said Tiny proudly.

"When did you build it?" we asked.

"Well, after the Great War I messed about in the interior, washing for diamonds in the north-west, hunting, digging for gold and that sort of thing, and then I thought it was time I settled down. I had already made one or two trips up the Rupununi river. In those days, we did it by boats up the rapids, and it took us sometimes a fortnight and sometimes a month according to the state of the river. I thought it was a nice sort of country — not too many people, you know — and I decided to make it my home. I came up the river looking for a place that was on high ground — so that I should be above the kaboura flies and wouldn't have difficulties with drainage — and which was also near enough to the river to enable me to bring all my stores and things up from the coast by boat. Of course, this house is really only a temporary one. I put it up in rather a hurry while I was laying out the plans and getting up all the materials to build a really fancy residence. I have still got all the plans in my mind and all the materials in the outhouse and I could start building it to-morrow, but somehow," he added, avoiding Connie's eye, "I don't ever seem to get started on it."

Connie laughed. "He's been saying that for twenty-five years," she said, "but you-all will be hungry, so let's sit down and eat." She moved over to the table and motioned to us to sit down. Around the table there were five up-ended orange boxes.

"I apologize for those terrible old things," said Tiny. "They're not nearly as good as the orange boxes we used to get before the war. You see, we once had chairs, but this floor is rather uneven and the chairs were always breaking their legs. Boxes haven't got any legs to break, so they last much longer, and really they are just as comfortable."

Meals with the McTurks are rather complicated. Connie has the reputation of being one of the finest cooks in Guyana and certainly the meal she put in front of us was magnificent. It started with steaks of lucanani, a delicate-tasting fish which Tiny regularly caught below the house in the Rupununi River. Roast duck followed — Tiny had shot them the previous day — and the meal ended with fruit from the trees outside. But competing for the food were two birds; a small parakeet and a black and yellow hangnest. They flew on to our shoulders begging for titbits, and as we were slightly unsure as to the correct way of behaving under these circumstances, we were a little slow in selecting morsels from our plates for the birds. The parakeet therefore decided to dispense with ceremony, perched on the rim of Jack's plate and helped herself. The hangnest adopted a different procedure and gave Charles a severe peck on the cheek with her needle-sharp bill to remind him of his responsibilities.

Connie however soon put a stop to this, chased the birds away and provided a specially cut-up meal for them in a saucer at the far end of the table. "That's what comes of breaking rules and feeding pets at the table. Your guests are pestered," she said.

As dusk fell towards the end of the meal, a colony of bats began to wake in the store-room and, leisurely and silently, flit across the living-room and out into the evening to begin hawking for flies. There was a scrabbling noise in the corner. "Really, Tiny," said Connie severely, "we must do something about those rats."

"Well, I did!" replied Tiny, a little hurt. He turned to us. "We had a boa-constrictor living in the passage which used to keep the place absolutely free from rats and then just because it once frightened one of the guests Connie made me get rid of it. And now look what's happened!"

After the meal, we left the table and settled down in hammocks to talk. Tiny told us story after story as night fell. He spoke of his early days on the savannahs when there were so many jaguar around Karanambo that he had had to shoot one a fortnight in order to preserve his cattle. He remembered how a party of outlaws from Brazil used to cross the border on horse-stealing raids, until he went over to Brazil himself, held up the gang at pistol point, took away their guns and burnt down their houses. We listened fascinated. The frogs and crickets started calling; the bats fluttered in and out, and once a large toad wandered in and sat blinking owlishly in the light of the paraffin lamp slung from the roof.

"When I first came up here," said Tiny, "I hired a Macusi Indian to come and work for me. After I had given him an advance, I found out that he was a piaiman or witch-doctor. If I had known that before, I wouldn't have hired him because witch-doctors are never good workers. Soon after he had taken the money, he told me that he wasn't going to work any more. I said that if he tried to go away before he had worked off the money I had given him, I would beat him. Well, he couldn't allow that to happen because he would lose face and then he wouldn't have any power among the Indians. I kept him until he had stayed long enough to clear off his advance and then I told him to go. When I did so, he told me that if I didn't pay him some more money he was going to blow on me, and if he did that, my eyes would turn to water and run out, I would get dysentery and all my bowels would drop out, and I would die. So I said 'Go ahead and blow on me', and I just stood up and let him blow. When he had finished I said, 'Well I don't know how Macusi blow, but I have lived a long time among the Akawaio and I am going to blow on you, Akawaio style.' So I puffed myself up and jumped around him and blew. As I blew, I told him that his mouth would shut up and he wouldn't be able to eat anything; that he would bend backwards until his heels and his head touched and that then he would die! Well, I then dismissed him and I never thought any more about it. I went up into the mountains hunting, and it was some days before I returned. Soon after I arrived, my head Indian came in and said, 'Massa Tiny, the man dead!' I said, 'There's plenty of people dead, boy. What man are you talking about?' 'That man you blow upon, he dead,' he said. 'When did he die?' I asked. 'The day before yesterday. His mouth shut up the same way as you said it would, he started to bend backwards and he died.'

"And he was right," said Tiny, concluding. "The man *had* died, just as I had said he would."

There was a long pause. "But, Tiny," I asked, "there must be more to the story than that. It couldn't have been merely coincidence."

"Well," said Tiny, looking mildly at the ceiling, "I had noticed a little sore on his foot and I knew that there had recently been two cases of tetanus in the village from which the man had come. Maybe that had something to do with it."

CHAPTER
FOUR
Egrets and Arapaima

Sharing breakfast with the parrot and the hangnest, we discussed with Tiny our plans for the day. Jack had decided that he should unpack the cages, troughs and feeding bowls before starting to catch any animals.

Tiny turned to us. "What about you-all, boys? Interested in some birds?" We nodded eagerly. "Well, come along with me, I might be able to show you a few not far from here," he said enigmatically.

Our walk with Tiny through the bush fringing the Rupununi river was an education in forest lore.

"You smell anything, boys?"

I sniffed, but could not detect anything. "No, I'm afraid I can't."

"There's some dead thing a few yards away from here smelling the place out. Nothing big, I don't suppose, but it might be interesting." He poked about in the undergrowth with his bush knife. "Here it is," he said, transfixing the corpse of a small lizard on the end of his knife for our examination. He threw it back in the bush and we walked on along the narrow path, Tiny occasionally lopping a dangling creeper with a swipe of his knife. He stopped again and pointed to the bole of a tree partially stripped of its bark.

"You know what that is?" Charles and I shook our heads. "Tapir. Couldn't be anything else." He surveyed it without bending down. "I reckon it was here about three days ago." He looked up into the trees. We followed his gaze without speaking. I could not see anything except the sun filtering through the tiers of emerald leaves fifty feet above us.

"I'm afraid I can't see anything up there either, Tiny," I confessed.

"Neither can I," he answered, "but you must be able to smell the howler monkeys. It's so strong they can't be far away; I was just trying to spot them."

I sniffed hard again. "I *think* I can smell them," I said doubtfully, "sort of . . ." I searched for a word to describe the faint odour that I was persuading myself I could detect. "Sort of musty?"

"Well yes, I suppose you could say that," Tiny admitted and strode off again along the path.

During the next half-hour of our walk, Tiny pointed out to us a hole in a dead tree-trunk trickling sawdust — the work of a carpenter bee — the spoor of an antelope, a magnificent purple orchid and the remains of an encampment where a party of Indians had come to fish in the creeks. Soon he branched off the main path and cautioned us not to talk. The undergrowth was thicker and we tried to match his silent tread.

The vegetation here was festooned with a creeping grass which covered all the bushes with bright green loops and hung down in veils between them. Ignorantly and carelessly, I tried to brush some away with the back of my hand, but I quickly withdrew it in pain, for the creeper was razor grass, the stems and leaves of which are armed with rows of tiny sharp spines. My hand was badly cut, and I said something louder than I should have done. Tiny turned round with his finger to his lips. Carefully picking our way through the tangle, we followed him. Soon the undergrowth became so thick that the easiest and most silent way of advancing was to wriggle forward on our stomachs, ducking under the razor grass.

At last he stopped and we drew alongside him. He carefully cut a small peephole in the thick blanket of razor grass which hung a few inches in front of our noses, and we peered through. In front of us lay a wide, swampy pond, its surface hidden by floating water-hyacinth which here and there was in flower, so that the brilliant green carpet was splashed with small areas of delicate lilac.

Fifteen yards beyond us the water hyacinth itself was obscured by the edge of an enormous flock of egrets which stretched across the centre of the lake and over to the other side.

"There you are, boys," whispered Tiny. "Any good to you?"

Charles and I nodded enthusiastically.

"Well, you won't want me," Tiny continued. "I'll get back for some breakfast. Good luck!" And he wriggled back soundlessly, leaving the two of us alone peeping through the razor grass. We looked again at the egrets. Two species were mingled in the flock; great egrets and the smaller snowy egrets. Through binoculars, we could see them raising their delicate filigree crests as they squabbled among themselves. Occasionally a couple would rise vertically in the air, sparring frenziedly with their beaks, only to subside as suddenly as they had risen.

Towards the far edge of the lake, we could see several tall jabiru storks standing head and shoulders above the other birds, their black naked heads and scarlet dropsical necks standing out vividly amid the pure white of the egrets. In the shallows on the far left hand side, there were hundreds of ducks. Some were lined up in pert regiments, each one facing the same way with military precision, others floated in squadrons on the pond itself. Close to us, a lily-trotter or jacana trod cautiously on the floating leaves of the water-hyacinth, its weight spread over several plants by its enormously elongated toes which made it lift its feet at each step with the action of a man in snow shoes.

Loveliest of all, within a few yards of us we saw four roseate spoonbills. As they dabbled busily in the shallow water, sifting the mud through their bills in search of small animal food, they looked ravishingly beautiful, for their feathers were suffused with the most delicate shades of pink. But every few minutes they lifted their heads to gaze around, and we saw that the ends of their bills were enlarged into flat discs which gave them a slightly comic look, oddly at variance with the grace and beauty of their bodies.

We set up the camera to begin filming this magnificent scene, but no matter where we placed it a small isolated bush in front of us impeded our view. We held a whispered council and decided to risk scaring the birds and advance across a few yards of lush grass to a spot underneath the bush which seemed just large enough to accommodate us both with the camera. If only we could reach it without causing alarm we should have a clear, uninterrupted view of all the birds on the lake — ducks, egrets, storks and spoonbills.

As quietly as possible we enlarged our peephole in the veil of razor-grass into a slit. Pushing the camera in front of us, we slowly wriggled out and across the grass. Charles gained the bush safely and I joined him. In slow motion, lest a sudden movement should scare the birds, we erected the tripod and screwed the camera into position. Charles had almost focused on the spoonbills, when I put my hand on his arm.

"Look over there," I whispered, and pointed to the far left of the lake. Sloshing their way through the shallows came a herd of savannah cattle. My immediate concern was that they might scare the spoonbills just as we were in a position to film them, but the birds took no notice. The cows came ponderously towards us, swinging their heads. In front of them walked a single leader cow. She stopped, lifted her head and sniffed the air. The rest of the herd stopped behind her. Then she advanced purposefully towards our little bush. When she was some fifteen yards away she stopped again, let out a bellow, and pawed the ground. From where we lay, she looked a very different animal from the gentle Guernseys of an English pasture. She bellowed again impatiently and brandished her horns at us. I felt very vulnerable lying there; if she charged she would have gone over the bush like a steamroller.

"If she charges," I whispered to Charles nervously, "she'll scare the birds, you know."

"She might also damage the camera and then we should be in a mess," whispered Charles.

"I think perhaps it might be wiser to retreat, don't you?" I said, with my eyes fixed on the cow. But Charles was already on his way, wriggling back to our razor-grass thicket and pushing his camera in front of him.

We sat well back in the bushes and felt foolish. To have come all the way to South America, the home of jaguar, venomous snakes and cannibal fish, and then to be frightened by a cow, seemed a little ignominious. We lit cigarettes and persuaded ourselves that for once discretion had indeed been the better part of valour, if only for the sake of our equipment.

After ten minutes, we decided to see if the cows were still there. They were, but they took no notice of us as we lay in our thicket. Then Charles pointed to a wisp of grass in front of us swaying gently in the breeze towards the cattle. The wind had changed and it was now in our favour. Emboldened by this, we once more wriggled out to the small bush and set up the cameras. For two hours we lay there, filming the egrets and the spoonbills. We watched and recorded a little drama in which two vultures found the head of a fish on the margin of the lake, only to be driven from their booty by an eagle, which then became so nervous of a counter-raid by the vultures that it could not settle down to eat the head and finally had to fly away with it. An hour before we had finished, the cows splashed their way back to the savannahs.

"What a wonderful sight it would be if all these birds took to flight," I whispered to Charles. "Edge your way out of the bush; I'll leap out on the other side, then as they take off stand up and film them wheeling against the sky."

With great care and moving very slowly so as not to startle the flock prematurely, Charles crept from under the bush and crouched by its side clutching his cameras.

"Right! Stand by!" I whispered melodramatically and with a shout I leapt from the bush waving my arms. The egrets took not the slightest notice. I clapped and shouted and there was still no movement. This was absurd. All that morning we had crept with infinite stealth through the bush, hardly daring to whisper lest we should frighten these supposedly timid birds, and now here we were standing shouting at the tops of our voices, yet the entire flock appeared totally unconcerned and our silence seemed to have been quite unwarranted. I laughed out loud and ran towards the edge of the lake. At last the ducks nearest to me took off. The egrets followed them and in a great surge the whole white flock peeled from the surface of the lake and swept into the air, their calls echoing over the rippling water.

Back at Karanambo, we confessed to Tiny our fear of cows.

"Well," he laughed, "they do get a bit skittish sometimes and I have had to run for it myself before now." We felt our reputations had not yet been irretrievably lost.

The next day Tiny took us to a stretch of the Rupununi river just below his house. As we walked along the banks, Tiny pointed out to us a series of deep potholes which riddled the soft tufa-like rock. He dropped a stone down one and an asthmatic belching echoed up from the pool in the bottom of the hole.

"One's at home," said Tiny. "There's an electric eel living in almost every one of these holes."

But I had another means of detecting the eels. Before we had left England, we had been asked to record the electric impulses of these fish on our tape recorder. The apparatus needed was simple — two small copper rods fixed in a piece of wood about six inches apart and connected to a piece of flex which could be plugged into our machine. I lowered this elementary piece of equipment into the hole and immediately heard on my small earphones the electric discharge of the eel recorded as a series of clicks, which increased in volume and frequency, rose to a climax and then subsided. This discharge is thought to act as a type of direction-finding device, for the eel possesses special sensitive organs all along its lateral line which enable it to detect the changes in electric potential caused by solid bodies in the water, and so to solve the problem of manoeuvring its six foot length among the rocks and crannies in the murky depths of the river. In addition to this minor semi-continuous discharge, the eel is also capable of delivering an immense high voltage shock with which it is supposed to kill its prey and which, it is said, is powerful enough to stun a man.

We moved on down to Tiny's landing and climbed into two canoes.

"Would you boys like to catch the biggest fish of your careers?" said Tiny as he started the outboard engine.

"Because a little creek along here is one of the best places I know for arapaima."

The arapaima is one of the largest freshwater fishes in the world and Tiny himself has caught several over ten feet long, though the record from Brazil is over fourteen feet. We chugged steadily up-river, passing on our way a tree colonized by a number of hangnest birds, their nests dangling like giant Indian clubs from the branches. Behind us we trailed hand-lines baited with spinning metallic lures in the hope that we might catch smaller fish before we reached the arapaima creek. Almost immediately I had a bite. Hauling in my line, I found a silvery-black fish, twelve inches long, and began removing the hook from its mouth.

"Watch your fingers," Tiny remarked idly. "That's a cannibal fish you've got there."

I dropped it hastily on the bottom of the boat.

"Don't do that, man," said Tiny, a little aggrieved, seizing a paddle and giving the ugly creature a clout which stunned it. "He might give you a nasty nip." He picked the fish up, and to prove his point stuck a piece of bamboo in its open mouth. The rows of triangular razor-edged teeth clashed shut on the bamboo, cutting it as cleanly as an axe-blow.

I watched appalled. "Is it really true that if a man fell in a shoal of those things, he would be hauled out a skeleton?" I asked.

Tiny laughed. "Well, I reckon that perai, as we call them, might make quite a mess of you, if you were silly enough to stay in the water once they started biting. It is usually the taste of blood that makes them attack in the first place, so I shouldn't go bathing if you've got an open cut. Luckily they don't like broken water, and so when you get out of a canoe and haul it up rapids you needn't worry, they are seldom there.

"Of course," he went on, "they sometimes attack unprovoked. I remember once getting into a canoe with fifteen Indians. We got in one at a time, and in doing so we had to put one foot in the water. No one except me had boots on. I was last in, and as I sat down, I noticed that the Indian in front of me was bleeding badly. I asked him if he was all right and he said that a perai had bitten him as he got in. It turned out that thirteen out of the fifteen had small pieces of flesh bitten clean out of their feet. None of them had cried out at the time, and no one had thought of warning the men coming afterwards. Still, I suppose that story tells you more about Indians than it does about perai."

Tiny swung the tiller and we left the main river and entered a small creek. "Well, here we are," he said, cutting the engine. "Let's have a try for arapaima."

As we drifted up the creek, Tiny cut up some small fish he had brought for bait, and fixed gobbets of the flesh on nine-inch iron hooks of his own forging. The hooks were attached to a long stout line, on the other end of which was tied a small log float. One by one as we moved slowly down the creek, Tiny threw the baited hooks and floats overboard. He paddled up to the bank and we looked behind us. In our wake stretched a line of six floats. We watched them carefully. Within ten minutes one of them started bobbing in the water. It then disappeared in a ripple and bobbed up again several yards away.

"We've got a bite," said Tiny enthusiastically, pushing out from the bank and starting to paddle feverishly. We drew alongside and Tiny, leaning over the side of the boat, seized the bobbing float. He jerked it upwards with all his strength and immediately the line whipped tight as the arapaima set off downstream. Suddenly the fish changed course and shot under the bows of the boat so that Jack and Tiny nearly capsized.

"Here, you take this thing," said Tiny, passing the line over to Jack and picking up a large harpoon from the bottom of the boat.

While he was still bent double, the arapaima broke above the surface of the water with an enormous splash, rocking the boat and almost throwing Tiny overboard. But before he could launch the harpoon it had disappeared again, diving beneath the boat and slewing it round with such force that Jack, holding the end of the line, was nearly pulled into the water.

The arapaima was now travelling fast along the bottom of the river, towing the canoe behind him and zig-zagging so that the cord was alternately slack and taut in Jack's hands.

"We must get him next time," said Tiny, "or else he may break the line and we'll lose him." As he spoke, the cord went limp and the arapaima shot from the surface of the water, giving us a glimpse of its enormous, milk-white under-belly. Instantly Tiny launched the harpoon into its flank with all the force he possessed. The shaft of the harpoon fell into the river, leaving the detachable head buried deep in the flesh of the fish and the cord to the harpoon head safe in Tiny's grasp. Now there were two lines to the fish, one in its mouth and one in its side, and by hauling on the two of them Jack and Tiny at last managed to raise the tiring monster close to the bows of the boat. Then, with a hammer, Tiny dealt the *coup-de grâce* and with a struggle they hauled the arapaima aboard.

It was an extraordinary-looking fish with a wedge-shaped head, an enormous mouth and a long olive-green body fading into cream and marked with red diamonds along its flanks. It was just over seven feet long and so heavy that it took two of us to lift it.

Tiny does not fish arapaima purely for sport. Its meat, though a little tasteless, is nevertheless good eating, and that evening as the monster hung suspended from a branch of a mango tree just outside the house Tiny stripped all the flesh from it, packing it in sacks.

"I'll dry that in the sun," he said, "and send it down to Teddy Melville. I know he likes a nice bit of arapaima and, poor chap, he is not as lucky as me in living near a decent fishing ground."

Two days before we were due to leave Karanambo, Tiny drove us across the open savannahs to see the annual round-up of his horses. For most of the year, they roam freely over the hundred square miles of his ranch. We arrived in time to see the last bunch being driven into the wooden corral by two whooping vaqueros. The herd that thundered round and round was composed of several dozen family groups, which until a few hours ago had been living independently on the savannahs. Each group was governed by one stallion and now in the corral these petty dictators found themselves side by side. Sometimes, inevitably, one would mingle with a rival's mares and then there would be a fight. Whinnying fiercely, the two would rear up, boxing with their forelegs, each seeking a chance to sink his teeth in the other's neck and mane. The engagements were short, but as the stallions broke away they lashed out viciously at one another with their hind legs.

We sat with Tiny on the corral fence as the bare-footed Indian vaqueros ran among the herd skilfully cutting out and lassoing the yearlings for branding. As each was caught and branded, Tiny kept tally in a small notebook.

After a short time, we left Tiny to his book-keeping and drove to a nearby part of the ranch where some of the horses were being broken in. First one was blindfolded, and then with extreme care a vaquero crept close, dropped a saddle on the horse's back and retreated just in time to miss a sudden wicked kick. Once the girths had been cautiously fastened, the vaquero mounted, the blindfold was removed and immediately the horse went mad. Rearing and bucking, it tried with everything in its power to remove the unnatural and hateful burden on its back.

While Jack and I watched, immensely impressed, Charles did his best to film the scene. His task was not easy for the vaquero had little control over the movements of his mount and several times flying hooves came unpleasantly close before Charles, with his eye glued to the viewfinder of his camera, could get out of the way.

Tiny arrived, astride a docile elderly mare. He watched

the vaquero desperately clinging to the wildly bucking horse.

"That ain't much good, boys," he remarked dryly. "That old nag has got no spirit in her. She's not even sun-fishing."

"Sun-fishing?" I asked.

"You know, jumping and arching her back, and at the same time twisting it sideways. All she is doing now is straight bucking, and there's no fun in that."

The horse had by now worked off most of its energy and relapsed into a nervous trot. The vaquero reined it to a halt and dismounted.

As we talked, Tiny sat lazily in the saddle of his horse, which stood with its head down amiably nibbling the grass.

"Your horse seems a nice quiet creature," I said.

"She's all right," answered Tiny. "You-all want a ride?"

The three of us politely suggested that one of the others should have the privilege of being the first to mount. Eventually we decided that Charles and I should record the event on film, and that therefore Jack should do the riding.

Tiny helped him up. The mare stood motionless and seemed totally unconcerned.

"I can't get my feet in these stirrups," Jack complained.

"Well, take your shoes off," laughed Tiny. "Those are Indian stirrups and they are only meant to be wide enough for a big toe."

Jack grasped the reins and cautiously muttered "Gee-up."

The horse looked at us mild-eyed, and nibbled a little more grass.

"Come on there," said Jack more boldly.

"Gee-up," he repeated loudly, digging his heels in its flanks.

The mare ambled slowly round a semi-circle.

"Film," I called severely to Jack, "is expensive stuff."

Charles looked up from behind his camera.

"What we've got so far," he said acidly, "would look tame in Rotten Row."

"I'll try again in a minute," said Jack apologetically, "but my saddle isn't quite right," and he brought his hands down to adjust it. As his fingers touched the horse's back, the animal suddenly bolted. Before Charles could get his eye to the camera, Jack and his mount were two hundred yards away going like the wind. Jack was still gamely vertical, but his stirrups were flying. They breasted a rise and headed straight for the corral fence. The horse will slow down now, I thought, and Jack will be all right; but at the last moment they veered right towards the entrance of the corral and it was a riderless horse that shot through the gate.

After an appalling length of time, we saw Jack rise from the ground through a cloud of dust and wave his arms bravely.

We leaped into the truck and drove to him as fast as we could. When we at last reached the corral, the vaqueros were still laughing uncontrollably, but poor Jack, leaning against a post, was in obvious pain.

We returned to Karanambo in the truck, driving as

carefully as we could, but each bump caused Jack agonies. Back at the house we decided that he had broken at least two ribs, and with advice from Dr. Jones in Georgetown over Tiny's radiophone, we bound up the damaged chest with bandages.

The next day we had to return to Lethem. Tim, with the help of Bolotov, had all the animals neatly crated. The following day a Dakota flew in with a lot of bulky freight and the pilot agreed that on the return journey he would take us and all the animals back to Georgetown.

As we flew over the forest, Jack sat on the caiman's crate with Robert the macaw bawling in his ear, and a long sticky tongue emerging through the slats of the anteater's cage at his feet.

"Well," he said, hugging his chest miserably, "if we come across any more horses, someone else can ride them. I'm going to stick to snakes."

CHAPTER
FIVE

The Mazaruni

The river Mazaruni rises in the highlands of the far west of Guyana, close to the Venezuelan border. For a hundred miles it winds round three parts of a huge circle before it breaks through the girdle of high sandstone mountains which enclose it and, over the short distance of twenty miles, descends thirteen hundred feet in a series of cascades and rapids which form an impassable barrier to river traffic.

The only land routes into the basin are long and arduous trails over the mountains, the easiest of them involving a three-day march through thick, difficult forest and a climb over a three-thousand-foot pass. The whole area, therefore, is virtually cut off from the rest of the Colony, and the fifteen hundred Amerindians who live there had, until a few years ago, remained isolated and relatively untouched by the civilization of the coast.

But the arrival of the aeroplane in Guyana completely changed the situation, for by amphibian plane it became possible to fly over the mountain barrier and land in the centre of the basin on a long, wide stretch of the Mazaruni River. This sudden accessibility might have had serious consequences for the Akawaio and

Arecuna tribes living there, so to prevent their possible exploitation, the Government declared the whole area an Amerindian reserve — forbidden country for diamond and gold prospectors and for travellers without permits. It also appointed a District Officer whose job it was to watch over the welfare of the Amerindians.

Bill Seggar held that post, and when we first arrived in Guyana he was, fortunately for us, paying one of his infrequent visits to Georgetown to buy six months' supply of food, trade goods, petrol and other necessities which had to be flown in to his station.

He was a tall, dark, heavily built man, with a deeply-lined face. Rather laconically, lest he should betray too much of the enthusiasm and pride which he felt for his province, he had told us of its wonders; of newly discovered waterfalls, of huge areas of unexplored forests, of the primitive "hallelujah" religion of the Akawaios, of humming birds, tapirs and macaws. He had estimated that he would have finished his business in Georgetown by the time we came back from our fortnight's visit to the Rupununi and had generously suggested that we might fly back with him to the basin.

So it was with great excitement that we now looked for Bill in Georgetown, to discover when his plane was leaving. We eventually ran him to earth in the bar of a hotel, gloomily staring at a glass of rum and ginger. He had bad news. The stores he had ordered were due to be flown in to the area by Dakota aircraft which normally landed on a small patch of open savannah near the eastern margin of the basin at Imbaimadai. This strip is usually serviceable throughout the long dry season, but during the rains it becomes waterlogged and useless. Theoretically, we should be able to use it now, in mid-April, but there had been a freakish outburst of rains which had converted the airstrip into a quagmire. Bill was going to fly into the area the next day by amphibian plane, land on the Mazaruni River just below the savannah at Imbaimadai, and then squat on the airfield, reporting its condition by radio day by day, so that as soon as it had dried out the freight planes could take off from Georgetown to bring in the essential stores. These supplies obviously must come first, but if they got in safely and if the strip was still dry, then we could follow as a last load. We finished our drinks moodily and said good-bye to Bill, wishing him luck when he took off next morning for Imbaimadai.

We waited in Georgetown, anxiously visiting the Department of the Interior each day for news of the airstrip. On the second day, we heard that the rain had stopped and that, given sun and no more rain, the airstrip should dry out and be serviceable in about four days. We spent those four days helping Tim Vinall settle the animals we had caught on the Rupununi in comfortable living quarters. The Agricultural Department had lent us a garage in the Botanic Gardens, which we quickly converted into a miniature zoo with cages stacked in tiers around its walls. Some of the bigger animals could not be accommodated, and very generously the Georgetown Zoo offered to take several of them, including the giant anteater, as temporary boarders. The caiman in its crate lay half-submerged in one of the canals in the gardens.

At the end of the four days, a wireless message was

received from Bill Seggar saying that all was well and that the freight plane could leave. All that day and the next, stores were ferried in to him. Then at last it was our turn.

We said our farewells to Tim, whose unenviable job it was to remain in Georgetown looking after the Rupununi animals, and once more with all our equipment we climbed into a Dakota aircraft.

Flying over rain forest is rather boring. Beneath us stretched an unbounded, featureless ocean of green. The myriad exciting forms of animal life which we knew it contained lay concealed beneath its dimpled green surface, though occasionally birds like flying fish skimmed above the crests of the trees. Once in a while we saw little clearings, dotted with tiny huts, like islands in the sea of forest.

After an hour, however, the prospect changed, for we were approaching the Pakaraima Mountains, which form the southeastern part of the Mazaruni's mountainous defences. The forests climbed on their flanks until, here and there, the slopes became so steep that no trees could grow upon them, and the mountain-side became a naked precipice of cream-coloured rock.

In a few minutes we sailed over these barriers which had proved so formidable to early travellers, and there below us wound the young Mazaruni River which even here was some fifty yards wide. Then, as if by a miracle, we saw below us in the middle of the forest a small patch of open savannah and towards one side of it a hut and two tiny white figures, which we knew were Bill and Daphne Seggar.

The Dakota circled and came down for a landing. Through no fault of the pilot's, it was a rather bumpy one, for the Imbaimadai airstrip has no tarmac runways, it is simply open country from which the larger boulders and the more obvious trees and bushes have been removed by Bill Seggar's Indian helpers.

The Seggars walked up to greet us. Both of them were barefoot, she tall and lithe in an athlete's woollen track-suit, he in a pair of khaki shorts and a shirt open to the waist, his hair still wet from a bathe in the river. Bill was highly relieved to see us, for with us in the plane we had the last of his essential stores; now, come what may, his provisions would last him through the rainy season. This he anticipated would not start for at least another month, and, all being well, we should be able to leave from the Imbaimadai airstrip four weeks hence.

"But," he said, "you can never tell. The rains may start again to-morrow. If they do, though," he added cheerfully, "we shall always be able to ship you out in instalments by amphibian plane at phenomenal cost."

We spent the night in the semi-ruined hut on the Imbaimadai airstrip, and the next morning Bill suggested that we should push on to the head waters of the Mazaruni and travel up the Karowrieng, one of the smaller tributaries of the main river, into uninhabited and relatively unexplored country. We asked what we might see.

"Well," said Bill, "nobody lives up there, so there must be plenty of wild life to interest you. There is also a pleasant waterfall, which I discovered a year or two ago, and some mysterious Amerindian cliff paintings which few people have ever seen and which no one seems to know much about. You might take a look at them too."

Bill was expecting further plane loads of goods, though these were not as vital as those he already had. The first load, however, was not due to arrive for another two days, and the next morning he suggested that he and Daphne should accompany us on the first day of our journey. Accordingly, the five of us climbed into a huge fourteen-foot dugout canoe fitted with a powerful outboard engine, which Bill habitually used in travelling about his area. A crew of six Amerindians came with us.

That day was a fascinating one for us; it was the first time we had had a close view of the forest. We travelled along a canyon of sunlight; beneath us the placid, translucent brown river, and on either side of us the vertical green walls of the forest. Purple-heart, green-heart and mora trees grew on the banks to a height of a hundred and fifty feet. Beneath their crowns, matted creepers and lianas dangled in a curtain which screened us from the interior of the forest. Nearer the ground, smaller bushes reached greedily outwards for the sunlight which was forbidden them in the gloomy depths of the forest. This leafy façade was not a uniform green, for as the rainy season was approaching some of the trees were sprouting fresh growths of amber-red leaves which hung limply downwards, forming clouds of vertical lines strikingly prominent among the riotous exuberance of the rest of the vegetation.

Here and there we saw a tree in flower. The most

common was one of medium height and naked except for its pink blossom, the colour of Japanese cherry, which fell into the river beneath and swept past us. Occasionally, we saw sprays of startlingly white or rich carmine orchids dangling down the emerald curtain. The muddy banks were lined with the bare, rotting trunks of dead trees, which had fallen into the river and had been dragged by the current so that they all pointed downstream in parallel ranks.

Once we passed a giant hundred-foot tree which had recently fallen. It was lying half-submerged, with the river racing through its branches, but it still trailed its lianas like the guys of a fallen mast.

We could not expect to see many animals from the boat as we travelled, for the noise of our engine echoing up and down the river would certainly frighten all the larger animals for miles around; but soon after we had started we flushed a pair of cormorants. They seemed unable to fly high enough to escape over the tops of the trees and unwilling to take shelter among the bushes on the bank, so they flew on ahead of us. After some time we had herded together a flock of over three dozen. They would fly several hundred yards in front of us, and settle on the projecting branches of a submerged, fallen tree. Then, as we approached, they would take off clumsily, splashing heavily with feet and wings. When they were finally airborne they flew so low that they touched wing-tips with their own reflections.

Twice we saw a turtle like a large yellow-green leaf lazily turning in the brown surface water. Kingfishers, large and small, darted around the banks, settling on branches and jerking their tails up and down in excitement.

Occasionally, and most miraculous of all, we saw a giant morpho butterfly, which flapped lazily out of the forest and across the river, tracing an erratic line of staccato blue flashes.

Two hours' journey brought us to a series of rapids. The river here tumbled over a wide barrier of rocks, which churned its amber brown into a creamy white. We unloaded the most delicate and easily damaged pieces of our equipment — cameras and recording machines — and carried them across a portage to the top of the rapids, and returned to help the boys drag the heavy canoe over the rocks. It was a hot and tiring job, but the Indians laughed over it and were convulsed with mirth when one of us clumsily lost a foothold and fell up to the waist in an unexpectedly deep cleft between the boulders. At last we hauled the canoe into the still, black pool which marked the top of the rapids, and once more we were on our way.

After another hour's travel, Bill told us to listen; above the noise of our engine we could hear a distant boom.

"My waterfall," he said.

Fifteen minutes more brought us to a bend in the river. The sound of the waterfall was now very loud indeed and Bill told us that it lay just round the curve. To go further up river would involve an arduous portage of the canoe round the falls and so we decided to make camp for the night on the bank. Bill and Daphne, however, could not stay with us, for they had to return to Imbaimadai to bring in the remaining plane-loads of stores.

Before they left, and while the Indians were clearing a camp site, they walked with us along the river bank to look at the waterfall. Guyana is rich in waterfalls. Only a few miles away south were the eight-hundred-foot Kaiteur Falls, so that in Guyanese terms, Bill's falls were negligible — a mere hundred feet high; yet as we rounded the bend in the river, they were a startlingly beautiful sight. A sickle-shaped, white sheet of foam thundered over an overhanging ledge and fell sheer into a wide, open pool at the base. We swam in the pool; we climbed among the tumbled boulders at the fall's base and scrambled round to the dank cavern underneath the falls, through which swifts were flitting.

Bill had christened his falls after the Maipuri — the colonial name for tapir — the tracks of which he had found on the river banks when he had first discovered them. Unfortunately we could not spend much time sight-seeing, for if Bill and Daphne were to get back to Imbaimadai before dark, they would have to return almost at once, so we retraced our steps to the Indians and the canoe.

Bill and Daphne, taking two of the Indians with them, set off again down river, leaving us with the promise that they would send the canoe back with an Indian in two days' time to collect us.

They had left us with four Indians to help carry our gear, wherever we might wish to go in the forest. They were all Akawaios, short, copper-coloured, cheerful men with straight, blue-black hair. As they all worked on Bill's station, they were partly Europeanized and wore khaki shorts and shirts and spoke a little pidgin English. The senior man, Kenneth, understood some, if not all, of the intricacies of the outboard engine, though we were to discover that his main method of dealing with any fault in the engine was to remove all its plugs and blow down them. His first lieutenant was named King George — a stocky shock-headed man with a permanent ferocious scowl. We understood from Bill that he was a head-man of a village farther down the river and had adopted this royal title himself. Efforts had been made to try to make him change his name to George King, but he had stoutly refused to do so.

While we had been looking at the falls, the four Indians had cleared a large area in the bush some fifteen yards square and had built a framework from saplings cut in the forest and bound together with pieces of bark and liana, over which they had stretched a large tarpaulin to protect us from a sudden rain-storm. Underneath this we were to sling our hammocks. A fire was already burning and water boiling. Kenneth came up to us with a gun in his hand and asked what sort of bird we would like for our supper. We suggested maam, the Lesser Tinamou, a small flightless bird rather like a partridge, which makes very good eating.

"Very well, sir," said Kenneth confidently, and disappeared into the forest.

An hour later, he returned with a large, fat maam, just as he had promised. I asked how he was able to find just the bird for which we had asked, and he told me that all Indians hunt by imitating bird calls. We had decided on maam, so he had gone into the forest and, moving stealthily, imitated the call of the maam, which is a long low whistle. After thirty minutes a bird had replied. Calling continuously, he had crept closer and closer to the bird and had finally shot it. Later, he told me a story about two Indians who went out in different directions hunting for maam. One whistled and got a reply. He crept nearer and nearer to the place from which the answering call was coming. Just as he was about to fire, he saw that it wasn't a bird which was replying to him at all, but the other Indian.

After supper, we climbed into our hammocks and settled down for our first night in the forest. Our fortnight on the savannahs had taught us something of the technique of hammock sleeping, but on the savannahs it had been hot throughout the night as well as the day, and here, high in the Mazaruni basin, the nights were very cold. I learnt that night that a hammock sleeper should take with him twice as many blankets as he would normally use in a bed, for he has to wrap himself below as well as above and the efficiency of a single blanket is thereby divided by two. It was so cold that, after an hour, I had to climb out of my hammock and put on all the spare clothes I had brought with me before I could get to sleep; even so, I passed a bad night.

I woke well before dawn, but as the sun rose I was amply rewarded, for the calls of macaws and parrots echoed over the river and a humming bird was already feeding on the blossoms of a creeper which hung down by the water's edge. It was a tiny, bejewelled creature, no bigger than a walnut, moving jerkily through the air. When it decided to feed from a flower, it hovered in front of it, flashing out its long, threadlike tongue and sipping the nectar from the depths of the flower. When it finished, it slowly reversed through the air on its rapidly beating wings and shot away in search of another blossom.

After breakfast, King George told us that the paintings Bill Seggar had mentioned lay two hours' march away in the forest. We asked him if he could lead us to them. He said that he had only been there once before, but that he was sure that he could find them again.

Jack, who was still feeling the ill effects of his fall on Tiny's ranch, decided to remain in camp and look for small animals in the forest nearby, so King George, with another of the Indians to carry our cameras, led us off into the bush. He went ahead unhesitatingly, cutting notches in the trees and bending over the heads of saplings to mark the route, so that we should not lose our way back. We were now in high, tropical rain forest. The great trees rose two hundred feet above us, most of them covered in plants which have the peculiar habit of not growing in earth, but of sending down long, aerial roots to draw nourishment from the humid air. Occasionally, on the forest floor, we came across a wide area scattered thickly with fallen, yellow blossoms, which made a carpet of colour in the gloomy forest. We looked up to see where they had come from, but all the trees rose so high above us that if it had not been for the fallen flowers we might never have guessed that any of them flowered at all.

In between the boles of the trees, there was a tangle of small saplings and creepers through which we had to cut a passage with our knives. We never saw a large animal, but we were well aware of the presence of innumerable tiny creatures around us, for the air was filled with the chirps and pipings of frogs, crickets and other insects.

After two hours' hard going, both Charles and I were very tired indeed. It was hot and muggy and we were soaked in sweat and very thirsty. We had not seen any water to drink since we left the river.

And then, suddenly, we came upon the cliff for which we had been searching. It rose vertically for several hundred feet and broke through the forest canopy, the shade of which had hitherto kept us in sweltering twilight. The rock and branches did not meet, and through the gap between them a shaft of sunlight struck diagonally down on to the white quartzite rock of the cliff, floodlighting the red and black paintings with which the rock was smothered. The sight was so impressive and so startling that weariness dropped from us and we raced excitedly to the foot of the cliff.

The paintings stretched for forty or fifty yards along its base and rose to a height of thirty or forty feet. The designs were crude, but many of them clearly represented animals. There were several groups of birds, probably maam, which Kenneth had hunted for us the previous evening, and many indeterminate quadrupeds. One seemed to us to be an armadillo, but then if we regarded the armadillo's head as a tail, the design became equally clearly a representation of an anteater. Another creature lay upside down, its feet in the air. At first we thought that this might represent a dead beast, but then we saw that it had two claws on its forelegs and three on its hind, the number possessed by a two-toed sloth. Above it, to corroborate our identification, was a thick, red line, obviously the branch on which the sloth should hang, but which, perhaps, presented difficulties in drawing to the unknown artist, who therefore painted it separately above the creature, to make his meaning clear. Among the animals were boldly painted symbols: squares, zig-zags, and strings of lozenges, the meaning of which we could not begin to guess at.

Most moving and evocative of all, interspersed between the animals and symbols, were hundreds of handprints. On the higher parts of the cliff they were in groups of six or eight, but near the base they were so numerous that they had been superimposed one upon the other to form almost solid areas of red paint. I placed my hand over several of them and found them all to be smaller than mine. At my request, King George made the same comparison; the prints fitted his hands exactly.

I asked King George if he could tell us what the paintings represented, but though he willingly made several wild suggestions for each animal we pointed to, his identifications were obviously just as tentative as ours. If we made alternative suggestions, he agreed and laughed and confessed he did not know; but one design we all agreed upon. "What's that?" I asked him, pointing to the outline of an upright, human figure which was very obviously male. King George was convulsed with laughter.

"He sporting," he said with a wide grin.

King George was most emphatic that he knew neither the significance nor the origin of the paintings. "They made long long time ago," he explained, "but not by Akawaio man." We found evidence of their antiquity, for here and there part of the hard rock had flaked away, taking with it a section of the paintings; the resultant scars were no longer fresh, but had weathered to the same shade as the rest of the cliff, a process which must have taken a great many years.

Their purpose, whatever it was, must have been an important one, for to place the designs so high on the cliffs, the artists must have gone to the labour of building special ladders. Perhaps the paintings were part of a magical ceremony connected with hunting, the Indian drawing the animal he desired and then registering his identity by leaving his hand print. Yet only one of the creatures, a bird, was shown as being dead and none appeared as being wounded, as they are so frequently shown in the Palaeolithic painted caves of France. For an hour Charles and I photographed the designs, building a crude ladder from saplings to enable us to reach the higher ones.

My thirst became overpowering, and as I came down the ladder for the last time, I noticed that water was dripping from the top of the overhanging cliff on to a boulder which was covered in thick, sodden moss. I hurried to the spot, squeezed lumps of the moss and moistened my mouth with the gritty, dark-brown water. Seeing me do this, King George disappeared among the cliffs to the left and within five minutes returned to say that he had discovered water. I followed him, clambering over the huge boulders that littered the base of the cliff A hundred yards to the left, a wide crack ran down the cliff face. As it approached the ground, it broadened and deepened into a small cave, the floor of which was formed by a deep, black pool of water.

In the back of the grotto, a vigorous stream of water tumbled into the pool; but the pool had no visible outlet. It presented such a startling appearance — this torrent spouting from the living rock and pouring into a seemingly bottomless pool which never overflowed — that for the moment I forgot my thirst. Surely such a pool could, to primitive minds, invest the cliff with a magical character. I remembered the grottoes of ancient Greece, into which sacrificial objects had been thrown to appease the gods, and plunged my arm into the water in the hopes of finding a stone axe-head; but the pool was so deep that I could only touch the bottom in the shallower part near the front margin and there I found only gravel. I tested the pool with a stick and found it to be over five feet deep.

My thirst quenched, I returned to the cliffs to tell Charles of the discovery. We sat and speculated as to what the paintings might mean and whether the grotto had any connection with them. By now the sun had disappeared over the crest of the cliff and the paintings had lost their theatrical lighting. If we were to regain camp that night we should have to start back immediately.

Regretfully, we gathered together the cameras and with a last look at the cliffs, enigmatic and shadowed, we turned our backs on them.

CHAPTER
SIX

Ants and Sloths

I had always imagined from reading travel books that the jungles of South America were swarming with animal life — that alligators infested the rivers; that monkeys gambolled in all the trees, and that at every other step a snake threatened the traveller with a hiss before sliding into the undergrowth. Yet on our walk to the cliff paintings and on our return to the river we saw no live creature of any sort. Although animals were not as abundant as I had believed, we nevertheless found plenty of evidence to show that the forest was not entirely deserted. Once, as we crossed a creek, we saw, printed across a white sandbank, a chain of footprints made by a tapir, and occasionally a harsh call from a parrot echoed through the forest, sounding clear above the monotonous droning chorus of insects. Our failure to see any of these creatures must have been due to the noise that we made, for though we walked as silently as we could, our progress no doubt created such a disturbance that all the big creatures fled in front of us and the smaller ones concealed themselves in the undergrowth. If we were to see any animals, we should obviously have to spend a great deal of time in silent, patient observation. We could not do that immediately, for we had arranged to return to Imbaimadai airstrip the next day and two Indians had already come up in the canoe to collect us.

We made the return trip in good time. Back at Imbaimadai, we found Bill and Daphne Seggar still awaiting more plane-loads of stores. There was nothing we could do to help and so next morning, at the Seggars' suggestion, we loaded the canoe with some of the goods that lay dumped on the airstrip and set off for Kamarang, Bill's permanent station at the mouth of the Kamarang River, sixty miles away down the Mazaruni.

We arrived in the late afternoon. The station, which is entirely Bill Seggar's own creation, consists of a small cluster of white wooden houses built in a clearing hewn with much labour out of the forest on the bank of the river. Behind the buildings, a long strip of rough ground has been cleared as the first stage in the construction of Kamarang's own airstrip, one of Bill Seggar's most cherished schemes. To our surprise we saw a tractor working on the strip hauling logs. It had been flown in to Imbaimadai in sections and, part by part, ferried down the river by canoe and reassembled.

The next morning, we began exploring the forest in a more leisurely way than had been possible on our journey to the paintings. We had only gone a few yards from the airstrip when we found a neat track some two inches wide, worn bare of vegetation, twisting through the scrub, dodging beneath fallen trunks and winding round bushes. It looked exactly like an English rabbit run, except that here and there were small semi-circular sections of leaves, some isolated, others in little piles, yet all fresh and green and obviously only recently cut. Laboriously we followed the track, but it became narrower and narrower and eventually dwindled to a thin intermittent line, only traceable by the leaf sections which had become more numerous.

The trail ended at the base of a small bush, or more exactly the skeleton of a small bush, for it had been stripped of its leaves. The stems were not roughly torn, but neatly sawn away. We were now certain that we had discovered the track of leaf-cutting ants. These creatures are one of South America's greatest scourges. In a few nights they are capable of turning a flourishing plantation into a cemetery of bare defoliated trees. The damage they cause is so enormous that when they invade the fields of an Indian village the inhabitants abandon their homes and move elsewhere rather than try to combat the inexorable insects, which will not cease work until all the crops are destroyed. There were no ants on the bush we had found, so we followed the path in the opposite direction. It became wider and wider, until finally, as we pushed through the thicker undergrowth, we were following a broad highway of smooth, brown earth, six inches wide.

By now, we had left the neighbourhood of the embryo airfield and were in high forest. A few hundred yards further on we came to the nest. Hitherto, the forest floor had been a springy, soggy carpet of rotting vegetation, but in front of us it was churned up into hummocks of yellow-brown earth over a roughly circular area about five yards across. In the centre, a moribund tree lurched drunkenly. Several dead saplings, seemingly killed by the subterranean tunnelling of the ants, still stood upright, suspended by their branches which were entangled with those of their living neighbours.

Close to where we stood, a stinkhorn fungus, a few inches high, erected its obscene spike which ended in a brown, foul-smelling cone hung around with a white lacy skirt. Here and there among the heaps of churned earth were mouths of tunnels about two inches across. The trail we had been following led to one of them and disappeared down it. Looking round, we saw that our track was only one of many. The nest was the hub of an enormous web, spokes of which stretched deep into the forest in all directions.

There was no sign of the ants themselves, though cut sections of leaves lay everywhere. This we expected, for we knew that leaf-cutting ants are nocturnal workers and spend most of the daytime deep in their nests, about their mysterious business.

I stamped hard near one of the holes, and within seconds the soldier ants of the colony climbed out, energetically waving their antennae, and looking for trouble. We knelt down to inspect them. They were over an inch long, with reddish-brown abdomens and enormously swollen, slightly hairy heads, armed with huge shear-like jaws. While Charles and I squatted on our heels discussing the ants, I learnt how powerful and effective their bite could be. I suddenly felt a sharp, severe pain in my calf and jumping up discovered that the jaws of one of the soldiers had pierced my stocking and made a clean cut in my flesh about a quarter of an inch long.

We wanted to see and film the inside of the nest, so we walked back to base and returned with a spade, thick rubber boots, and cameras. After I had dug two shovelfuls the ants swarmed out in thousands, and within seconds my boots were covered with enraged soldiers, viciously sinking their jaws into the rubber. I thought I was well protected, but before long some of the more enterprising individuals were climbing higher up my boots and nearer my unprotected flesh. Ten minutes later I had to retreat and brush off all my attackers before starting again.

After half an hour's hard work, I had excavated a considerable section of the nest and at last found what I had been searching for — a chamber some three feet below the surface. On its floor were scattered some leaf sections similar to those which had originally led us to the nest, but most of the interior was filled with a spongy honey-coloured ball. I brought some of it out on the end of my spade and looked at it closely, for this material was the answer to a problem that had puzzled naturalists for many years — the problem of how the ants used the vast quantities of leaves which they cut with such industry.

Bates, the nineteenth-century naturalist who explored the Amazon, decided that the ants used the leaves to thatch their nests. Enormous though these nests are, however, this solution could not possibly account for all the leaves that a colony cuts each night. It was ten years later that Belt, working in Nicaragua, made the remarkable discovery that the ants masticate the leaves and convert them into a sort of compost on which to grow fungus for food.

I now held some of that compost in my hand.

I looked closely at it and could just distinguish in the crumbling earthy mass a maze of thin, white, fungal hairs. These hairs, under some unknown stimulation by the ants, produce small capsule-like fruits which provide food for the millions of individuals working in the nest. Strangely enough, this species of fungus is never found anywhere else in the forest; as far as is known, it exists solely in the ants' nests. Maybe, it has been produced from an independent species of fungus by a process of selective cultivation analogous to that which has produced the improved varieties of flowers and vegetables of our own gardens. To the ants it is extremely precious, for it is their only food supply. Scientists, called in to combat the ants, have discovered that although fumigation and other severe measures leave the colony relatively unharmed, the whole nest of ants will die if the fungus gardens are destroyed. The fungus indeed is so vital to the life of the colony that young queen ants, flying from the nest to found new colonies, have to carry with them in their mouths a tiny pellet of the fungus from the parent nest with which to plant new gardens.

Having filmed the inside of the nest, we now wanted to take pictures of the ants in the process of devastating a tree. But there was one great difficulty: we knew that nearly all the cutting was carried out during the night. If we were lucky enough to find them at work, we should have to film them by the light of magnesium flares. These only burn for two minutes at a time, and filming in two-minute spasms would complicate the already difficult task of micro-cinephotography.

The nights immediately after our discovery of the

nest were rainy and unsuitable for filming and it was not until a week later that we had our first sight of the ants actually at work. Charles and I were staying in an Indian village farther down the Mazaruni River. The head-man had invited us to sling our hammocks in a low, circular hut with a domed roof thatched with palm leaves. We had both been asleep for some time, when I was awakened by something crawling over my face. Sleepily, I brushed it off and turned over, thinking it to be some stray insect that had flown in from the forest, but soon there were more to be brushed away and within a few minutes I was wide awake. Small creatures were crawling all over my arms and neck. Above me I heard a vague, unidentifiable, rustling noise.

Shaking myself, I reached beneath my hammock for my hunting torch. In its light I saw that my hammock ropes were being used as a highway for laden leaf-cutting ants, which were staggering down the rope carrying their burden of leaves and crawling over me in the mistaken belief that I could provide them with a route back to the ground. I followed the line of insects with the beam of my torch and saw that they were at work in the roof of the hut which had only recently been patched up with new green palm leaves. The Indians having carefully and industriously repaired the roof, the ants were now busily removing it piecemeal. This was our chance to obtain the film we wanted.

I shook Charles's hammock and explained the situation. Together we went over to our equipment and in the light of torches found the camera, the stand, the correct lenses and the flares. The ants were swarming in both directions along one of the hut posts and the hammock route was a mere tributary compared to this main stream.

When the camera was at last set up, I stuck the flare on the end of a pole and lit it. Immediately the whole village was flooded with light as bright as day. Two things happened: first, the population of the village woke up with a start and leapt from their hammocks, the more naïve under the impression that some frightful calamity had befallen them; the more sophisticated, to see what new magic their visitors had brought with them.

This was frustrating enough, for while we tried to explain to the milling crowd around us what was happening, photography was impossible and our valuable flare — for we only had a few with us — was being wasted.

But the second result was worse, for within seconds of the flare being lit the ants had stopped work and had almost entirely evacuated the roof. When at last Charles was able to concentrate on the task of filming, there were no ants to be found.

We waited hopefully for an hour, but they did not resume work again that night. Nevertheless our flares served one useful purpose; my sleep for the rest of the night was undisturbed.

Obviously the task of getting pictures of the ants at work was going to be a difficult one; but from what I had seen only too briefly, it was an extremely dramatic sight which would be well worth a great deal of trouble to film.

Success came to us about a fortnight later. We had risen

just after dawn and were walking in the forest when, to my delight, I saw a line of ants wobbling unsteadily along a trail with discs of leaves several times their own size clasped upright between their jaws and held over their backs. Their alternative name, "parasol ant", seemed very appropriate. We followed the trail back in the direction from which the ants were coming, and within a few yards found the bush which they were ravaging.

Half of it had already been reduced to bare stems and on its few remaining leaves the ants were still at work. They used their jaws not as scissors but rather as tin-openers, twisting their heads from side to side so that the top jaw did no cutting but provided purchase on which the lower jaw could act.

Each ant began at the margin of the leaf and cut round in an arc, twisting its head furiously, until it came to the last few cuts with which the section would be severed from the leaf. This was a critical moment. There was a danger that the section might fall to the ground and plainly this was no part of the ant's plan. As the last cuts were made, the ant held the section firmly with its two front legs, gripping the main leaf with its other four. Grimly it hauled the dangling section up on to the main leaf, holding its booty vertically with its forelegs. It then tucked its head down between its front legs so that its jaws were almost horizontal beneath its abdomen. Finally, it closed its jaws on the section, raised its head and hoisted the leaf disc into its correct ceremonial position — upright above its body, like a flag.

Though we watched them for over an hour, there appeared to be no co-operation between the ants;

indeed, they often impeded one another by crawling unconcernedly over a leaf section as it was being cut and even by riding on the severed disc that a fellow-worker was carrying. The task of cutting the section and transporting it perhaps a quarter of a mile was one which each ant tackled alone and unaided. By the time the sun was fully up, the bush was completely bare and the last flag-bearer had descended the main stem on to the ground and was staggering back along the trail to the nest with its enormous burden.

Though we never saw the ants in the act of cutting again, we came across their distinctive trails every day that we were in the forest. Finding many of the other equally common insects, however, was a much harder task, for the colour and shape of the majority of them so closely matched their background that they were almost invisible. This camouflage, as in a human war, enables the hunter to wait in ambush as well as the hunted to lie in concealment.

One of the most voracious of all insect hunters in the forest is the mantis. We had seen and filmed a member of this widespread family when we had been in Africa. Though only a few inches long, it had looked the personification of ferocity. Its head, the shape of an inverted triangle, swivelled in all directions as the creature searched for its prey. It held its forelegs, in an attitude of hypocritical piety, clasped in front of it as if in prayer. Only when it shot these legs forward to seize a grasshopper did we see that their function was not devotion but aggression: they were grappling irons, armed with wicked spikes.

That was the mantis with which we were familiar — in all conscience, a sufficiently bizarre creature — but I was unprepared for its extraordinary relation which Jack found a few yards away from the Seggars' house. He brushed against a bush with his arm and a large mantis whirred into the air, flew a few yards and settled on another bush. As it folded its wings, it seemed to disappear. We had to search very carefully to rediscover it, so closely did it resemble the leaves around it.

Its wing-covers, unlike those of a common mantis which are brown and narrow, were olive-green and enormously enlarged. Above its head and thorax it bore a similarly coloured plate which combined with the huge wing-covers to form the outline of a leaf: it looked like a common mantis carrying above itself a permanent, camouflaging shield. We were only able to spot the insect because it had extended one of its spiked forelegs beyond the shelter of its disguise to grip the edge of a leaf and had so betrayed its presence.

Jack caught it with a deft swipe of his net. For several days we filmed it making meals from grasshoppers and butterflies and displaying the same cold-blooded ferocity as its African relatives. Having seized an unsuspecting grasshopper, it held the doomed and squirming insect in its crooked forelegs and methodically masticated its victim's abdomen, starting at the rear and working towards the head as though it were eating corn from the cob. When it reached the base of the grasshopper's wings, it got them entangled in its jaws. It lifted its head and, in exactly the same way as the African mantis, deliberately spat out the tasteless wings before continuing with its meal.

Beautifully camouflaged though this insect was, it was surpassed by a type of grasshopper which we found a few days later. To say that it bore a resemblance to a leaf is an understatement. This astonishing insect, nearly three inches long, carried its wing-covers upright like a butterfly, but instead of being brilliantly coloured, they were light green and marked in perfect imitation of a leaf. A false midrib ran from just above its head to the far tip of its wing. Here and there it was blotched with spots of rusty brown in just the same way as the dying leaves in the humid forest are patterned with mould. The two wing covers were marked identically, and near the top margin a small transparent patch on each coincided exactly, so that when the covers were folded it seemed that the imitation leaf was pierced by a hole.

Unfortunately, we never had these two extreme examples of insect camouflage in captivity at the same time. It would have been fascinating to confront the two and see which disguise was the more effective.

We recruited two of the Akawaio Indians who worked on the station to accompany us on our jaunts. Their eyes were more skilled than ours in spotting the smaller animals and they also knew the forest so intimately that they could take us to flowering trees that might be attracting humming birds and to others in fruit that might be visited by flocks of parrots or troops of monkeys.

Our first major success, however, was scored by Jack. We were walking through the forest not far from the airstrip, picking our way through spiny creepers. We paused at the base of one of the largest trees we had so far found. From its branches high above us hung thick lianas in immobile contortions. If we could have concentrated several years of the lianas' movements into a few minutes, we should have seen them twisting and writhing, strangling both themselves and the trees from which they hung. Jack looked up into the tangle.

"Is there anything up there, or is it my imagination?" he said softly.

I could see nothing. Jack explained more carefully where I should look and at last I saw what he had spotted — a round grey shape hanging upside-down from a liana. It was a sloth.

Sloths are incapable of rapid movement and, for a change, there was no risk that it would career off and be lost in a few seconds in the higher reaches of the forest roof. There was enough time for us to decide that Charles should film the capture, that Jack's ribs were still painful enough to prevent him doing anything strenuous, and that I, therefore, should be the one to climb up and bring the mysterious creature down.

The ascent was not difficult, for the dangling creepers provided an abundance of holds. The sloth saw me coming and in a slow-motion frenzy began climbing hand-over-hand up its liana. It moved so slowly that I was able to overhaul it with ease and forty feet above the ground I caught up with it.

The sloth, about the size of a large sheepdog, hung upside down and stared at me with an expression of ineffable sadness on its furry face. Slowly it opened its mouth, exposing its black enamel-less teeth, and did its best to frighten me by making the loudest noise of which it is capable — a faint bronchial wheeze. I stretched out my hand and, in reply, the creature made a slow, ponderous swing at me with its foreleg. I drew back and it blinked mildly, surprised that it had failed to hook me.

Its two attempts at active defence having been unsuccessful, it now concentrated on clinging firmly to the liana. Loosening its grip was not easy, for my own position was somewhat precarious. Holding on to my own liana with one hand, I reached over with the other and tried to detach the sloth. As I prised loose the scimitar-sharp claws on one foot and began work on the next, the sloth, very sensibly and with maddening deliberation, replaced its loosened foot. At no time did I manage to get more than one limb free at a time. I continued for five minutes in this way, not substantially helped by the ribald suggestions that Jack and Charles shouted up to me. Plainly, this one-handed struggle could go on for ever.

Then I had an idea: close by me hung a thin, crinkled liana, nicknamed by the Indians "granny's backbone". I called down to Jack and ask him to cut it loose near the ground. I then pulled the severed end up to me and dangled it near the sloth as I unfastened each of its legs. The animal was so determined to grasp anything within reach that, limb by limb, I was able to transfer it to the smaller liana. That done, I gently lowered the liana so that the sloth, clinging obligingly on the end, slowly descended straight into Jack's arms. I clambered down.

"Nice, isn't it?" I said, "and it's a different species from the one I remember seeing in the Zoo."

"Yes, it is," Jack replied mournfully. "The one in London is a two-toed sloth. It has been there for several years, feeding quite happily on apples, lettuce and carrots. This one here is the three-toed species. You've never seen it in London for the simple reason that it will only eat cecropia plant, and while there's plenty of cecropia in the forest here, there's none to be got in London."

We knew therefore that we had to release it, but before doing so, we decided to keep it for a few days so that we could watch and film it. We carried it back and put it on the ground near the base of an isolated mango tree, near the house. Without a branch to hang from, the sloth had the greatest difficulty in moving at all. Its long legs splayed out and it was only by laboriously humping its body that it managed to drag itself across the few yards that separated it from the bole of the mango tree. Once the creature was there, however, it clambered gracefully up the trunk and contentedly suspended itself beneath one of the boughs.

Every feature of its body seemed to have been modified in some way to suit its inverted existence. Its grey, shaggy hair, instead of flowing down from its backbone towards its stomach as in any normal creature, was parted along its belly and flowed towards its spine. Its feet were so extensively adapted to act as hangers that they had lost all sign of a palm and the hook-like claws appeared to project straight from a furry stump.

A wide circle of vision is obviously very necessary when hanging in the tree tops, and the animal had a long neck which enabled it to twist its head through almost a full circle. The sloth's neck bones are of considerable interest to the biologist, for whereas nearly all mammals, from mice to giraffes, have only seven bones in their neck, the three-toed sloth has nine. It is tempting to conclude that this also is a special adaptation for an upside down life. Unfortunately for the theorists, however, the two-toed sloth, which lives in exactly the same manner, and which can perform similar feats of neck mobility, has only six neck-bones, one less than nearly all other mammals.

On the third day, we noticed our sloth craning forward in an endeavour to lick something on its hip. Curious, we looked closer, and to our astonishment saw that it was caressing a tiny baby, still wet, that must have been born only a few minutes earlier.

The fur of a sloth is supposed to support a growth of microscopic plants, giving the creature a greenish-brown tinge which is of considerable value to it as camouflage. The birth of this baby, however, did not corroborate this, for the infant could not yet have accumulated its own garden in its coat, and yet it was exactly the same colour as its mother. Indeed, when it had dried we had the greatest difficulty in distinguishing it as it nestled in its mother's shaggy fur, occasionally groping along the length of her enormous body to suck from the nipples in her armpits.

We watched the pair for two days, the mother tenderly licking her baby, sometimes detaching one of her legs from the bough above her to support her tiny offspring. The birth seemed to have robbed her of her appetite and she no longer took slow bites from the cecropia which we tied to her tree. Rather than run the risk of her going hungry, we carried the two back to the forest. There we hooked her on to a liana, and with her baby peering at us over her shoulder she started to climb upwards.

When we returned to the spot an hour later to make sure that all was well, mother and child were nowhere to be seen.

CHAPTER SEVEN

The Kako and Clarence

Soon after we released the sloth, Bill and Daphne Seggar returned to Kamarang, their canoe piled high with stores. There still remained a large dump of supplies on the airstrip at Imbaimadai and Kenneth was to return the next day in the canoe to bring down another load. Jack had decided that he should remain at Kamarang for another few days and concentrate on collecting animals in the immediate neighbourhood. But part of our filming schedule was to record something of the everyday life in an Amerindian village and Bill suggested that, as engine-fuel was at a premium, Charles and I should travel up-river with Kenneth, land at one of the villages, and stay there for a time.

"I should go to Wailamepu first," Bill said. "It's a short way up the Kako River, a tributary of the Mazaruni. One of the villagers is a bright young lad named Clarence who once worked for me here and who consequently speaks quite good English."

"Clarence?" I asked. "That seems rather an odd name for an Akawaio Indian."

"Well, the old religion of the Indians was 'Hallelujah', an odd, debased version of Christianity which arose in the southern part of Guyana in the early nineteenth century; but Seventh Day Adventist missionaries converted the inhabitants of Wailamepu village and in the process re-christened them with European names.

"Of course," he went on, "the old names are still used among themselves, but I don't think you will find many Indians who will tell you their Akawaio name." He laughed. "They seem to be able to combine their old beliefs quite conveniently with the new ones taught by the missionaries and will shift from one to the other whenever it suits them.

"The Adventists teach, for example, that you should not eat rabbit. Of course, there are no rabbits here but a large rodent called a labba is roughly equivalent. Unfortunately, labba-meat has always been one of the favourite foods of the Indians and forbidding it was quite a blow to them. There is a story that a missionary once came across one of his Indian converts cooking a labba over a fire. He told the Indian how sinful it was.

"'But this is not labba,' the Indian said, 'this is fish.' 'No fish has two big front teeth like that,' replied the missionary crossly, 'you speak nonsense.' 'No, sir!' said the Indian. 'You know how, when you first came to this village, you say my Indian name is bad name, and you sprinkled water over me and say my name is now John. Well, sir, I walk in the forest to-day, I see labba and I shoot 'im, and before he die, I throw water over him and I say "Labba be bad name, you be fish." And so now I eat fish, sir.'"

* * *

The next morning we set off for Wailamepu with Kenneth and King George. The outboard engine was working perfectly and in two hours we reached the mouth of the Kako River. After fifteen minutes' journey up the Kako, we saw a path running up the river bank into the forest. At its foot, by a muddy landing, were moored several canoes. We stopped our engine, disembarked and walked up the path to the village.

Scattered around a sandy clearing were eight rectangular ridge-roofed huts, raised on short stilts. Their walls and floors were of bark, and they were thatched with palm leaves. Women, some in filthy torn cotton frocks, others wearing only the traditional bead apron around their loins, stood at the doors of the houses and watched us. Scraggy chickens and mangy dogs wandered in and out of the huts and tiny lizards skittered from beneath our feet as we went.

Kenneth led us up to an old, genial man sitting in the sun on the steps of his house. He was naked except for a pair of tattered, heavily-patched shorts which had once been khaki.

"This, head-man," said Kenneth, and he introduced us. The head-man spoke no English, but through Kenneth he welcomed us and suggested that we should stay in a derelict hut at the far end of the village, which was used as a church when the missionary came to the district. Meanwhile, King George had enlisted the aid of some of the village boys, and between them they had brought all our baggage from the boat and laid it in a pile near the church.

We walked back to the river with Kenneth and King

George. Kenneth wrestled with the outboard engine. At last it started and the boat surged away from the bank. "I come back one week's time," yelled Kenneth above the roar of the engine as he disappeared down-river.

Most of that day we spent in unpacking our gear and constructing a little kitchen outside the hut. Later we wandered about the village endeavouring not to appear too inquisitive too early, for it seemed hardly polite to start peering into huts and taking photographs until we had got to know the villagers. We soon discovered Clarence, a cheerful man in his early twenties, sitting in his hammock, busy weaving an elaborate piece of basket-work. He welcomed us with genuine sincerity but made it clear that at that moment he was too busy to do more than exchange a few words.

We returned to the church in the late afternoon and began thinking of making a meal.

Clarence appeared at the door.

"Good night," he said with an expansive smile.

"Good night," we replied, having been forewarned that this was the normal evening greeting.

"I bring you these t'ings," he said, putting down three large pineapples on the floor. He sat down and settled himself comfortably in the doorway, his back against the doorpost.

"You come from long way?" We admitted that we did.

"An' why you come here?"

"Our people, far far away across the sea, do not know anything about the Akawaio on the Mazaruni. We bring all kinds of machine to take pictures and sounds, so that we can show our people how you make cassava bread and woodskin canoes and all things like that."

Clarence looked incredulous.

"You t'ink anyone far away wish to know those t'ings?"

"Yes, for sure."

"Well, the people here will show you if you really wish," said Clarence, still slightly doubtful. "But please, you show me all these t'ings you bring."

Charles produced the camera and Clarence peered down the viewfinder with delight. I demonstrated the tape recorder. This was an even greater success.

"These fine t'ings," said Clarence, his eyes gleaming with enthusiasm.

"There be one other thing we come for," I said. "We wish to find all kind of animals: birds, snakes, every kind of thing we want."

"Ah ha!" said Clarence. "King George told me 'bout one man you leave bottom-side at Kamarang, who able catch snakes and get no fear at all. That true t'ing that King George say?"

"Yes," I replied. "My friend he catch all things."

"You catch snakes too?" inquired Clarence.

"Well, yes," I replied modestly, anxious not to let pass this chance of gratuitous prestige.

Clarence pressed the matter.

"Even the kind that bite bad?"

"Er — yes," I said, rather uncomfortably, hoping that I would not be drawn too deep into discussion about the matter. The fact was that whenever snakes appeared Jack, as Curator of Reptiles, was the person *ex officio* who caught them. My achievements had been limited to once picking up a very small, timid, non-poisonous python in Africa.

There was a long pause.

"Well, good night," said Clarence brightly, and he disappeared.

Charles and I settled down to our meal of tinned sardines followed by one of the pineapples which Clarence had brought us. Darkness fell and we climbed into our hammocks and prepared for sleep.

We were wakened by a loud "Good night!" I looked up and found Clarence with the entire population of the village standing around the door of the hut.

"You tell these people what you tell me," demanded Clarence.

We got up, repeated our stories, showed the light of the paraffin lamp in the camera viewfinder and played the recorder.

"We all sing now," announced Clarence, organizing the rest of the villagers into an orderly group. Without the least trace of enthusiasm, they chanted a long dirge in which I thought I could detect the word "hallelujah". I remembered what Bill had told me.

"Why you sing Hallelujah chant, I thought this be Adventist village?"

"We all Adventists," explained Clarence airily, "and sometimes we all sing Adventist song, but when we *really* happy," he added, leaning forward conspiratorially, "we sing Hallelujah." He brightened. "Now we sing Adventist song because you ask for it."

I recorded the chant and when it was finished, played

it back to the villagers on a small speaker. They were entranced and Clarence insisted that now each member should perform a solo. Some sang guttural dirges and one man produced a flute, made from the shin-bone of a deer, on which he played a simple tune. This lengthy concert slightly embarrassed us, for we only had a limited number of tapes and our machine, being a small, lightweight, battery-operated model, did not carry an erasing device. If I recorded everything, I might waste all my valuable tapes on these relatively worthless party-pieces and when I heard genuine spontaneous material there would be no tapes left. So I tried to record the minimum of each performance necessary to convince each singer that justice had been done to him.

After an hour and a half, the music came to an end and the villagers sat around the hut chattering in Akawaio, fingering our equipment and clothes and laughing among themselves. We could not join in the conversation and Clarence was involved in a heated discussion with another man outside the hut. We sat, ignored, wondering what was the polite thing to do and resigning ourselves to getting no sleep that night.

Clarence stuck his head in the door.

"Good night," he said, beaming.

"Good night," we replied, and all twenty of our guests without a word got to their feet and trooped out into the night.

Early next morning, two young Indian boys came into our hut as we sat at breakfast. They were naked except for red-brown loincloths and they carried a tame parrot.

"You want?" one asked with a shy smile. He handed me the bird which promptly bit me sharply on the hand. We accepted it gratefully and gave them a reward. I asked their names.

"Kaltun" and "Codrice" they replied. I enthusiastically noted these in my diary, under the impression that we had discovered some genuine Akawaio names. I later found out to my disappointment that the missionary's taste in names was somewhat eclectic and that the two boys had in fact been christened "Carlton" and "Goodridge".

We felt that the boys' gift meant that we were now accepted in the village and that therefore we could begin our filming.

The main occupation of the women was the making of cassava bread, thin flat cakes of which lay drying in the sun on the roofs of the houses and on special racks. They grew the cassava in plots between the village and the river. We filmed the women as they dug up the tall plants and removed the starchy tubers from among the roots. These they peeled and grated on a board studded with sharp fragments of stone. The juice of cassava contains a lethal poison — prussic acid — and to remove it a woman loaded the soggy, grated cassava into a matapee, a six-foot tube of extendable basket-work closed at one end with loops at top and bottom. When it was full she hung the matapee on a projecting beam of a hut. She passed a pole through the bottom loop and attached it to a rope tied to the hut post. Then she sat on the free end of the pole, and the laden matapee, squat and fat, stretched so that it became long and thin. In doing so, it squeezed the cassava and the poisonous juice trickled out at the bottom.

The dry cassava was then sieved and baked. Some of the women used a flattened stone, but others employed a cast-iron circular plate, exactly the same as is used in Wales and Scotland in making girdle cakes. The flat disc of cassava bread having been cooked on both sides was put outside to dry.

Having filmed the whole process, I felt we should sample some of the finished product. It was dry and tasteless, though doubtless filling. The Indians themselves probably agree with this verdict, for they seldom eat the bread without dipping it in a highly spiced gravy made with the tiny red chili-peppers from bushes growing near the village. It is so strong that it will remove the skin from the top of your mouth if you are not used to it.

Clarence had been our general aide throughout the filming, translating our requests to the performers to move into the sunlight, and reassuring them that our cameras were not in the least harmful. We packed up our gear and Clarence wandered off towards his hut.

He came back at a run.

"Quick, quick, Dayveed!" he yelled, waving his arms wildly. "I find t'ing for you to catch."

I ran after him to a log lying in a patch of low scrub close to his hut. By the side of it, I saw a small, black snake, about eighteen inches long, slowly swallowing a lizard.

"Quick, quick, you catch 'im," Clarence cried enthusiastically.

"Well . . . er, I think we should film him first," I said, procrastinating. "Charles, come quickly."

The snake, unconcerned by all the excitement, continued with its meal. The head and shoulders of the lizard had already disappeared and we could just see the tips of its front toes, pressed back against its body, projecting out of the corners of the snake's mouth. In girth, the snake was about a third of the size of the lizard, and to accommodate its enormous meal, the snake had unhinged its lower jaw. Even so, it had to open its mouth so wide that its little black eyes almost popped out of its head.

"Eh!" called Clarence to the world at large. "Dayveed, he goin' to catch this bad snake!"

"Is this a *very* bad one?" I asked Clarence nervously.

"I don' know," he replied with relish, "but I t'ink 'e terrible bad."

Meanwhile Charles was already filming. He looked up over his camera. "I'd like to help," he said smugly, "but I must record this unique exhibition of gallantry."

By now, the snake had reached the hind legs of the lizard. It was not eating it so much as crawling over and around its victim, for the lizard had remained in exactly the same position relative to the ground, while the snake slowly advanced towards its victim's tail. It did this by wrinkling its body into zig-zags and then stretching straight in rather the same way as one threads a cord into pyjama trousers.

Most of the villagers had assembled in an expectant circle. The last tip of the lizard's tail disappeared and the little snake, grossly distended, began to crawl heavily away.

I had no excuse for further delay. Taking a forked

stick I jabbed it down astride the snake's neck, so that the reptile was pinned to the ground.

"Quick, Charles," I said, "I can't do anything more unless you have a collecting bag."

"Here's one," Charles replied cheerfully, pulling a small cotton bag from his pocket. He held it open. With great distaste, I put a thumb and forefinger round the snake's neck, picked it up and dropped the wriggling creature into the bag. I heaved a sigh of relief and in as casual a manner as I could manage walked back to our hut.

Clarence and the spectators trotted behind.

"Sometimes maybe we find a big, big, bushmaster snake and then you show us how you catch *that* t'ing," he chattered enthusiastically.

It was a week before I could show my capture to Jack.

"Non-poisonous," he said tersely, handling it with complete unconcern. "You won't mind if I let it go, will you?" he added, "because it is very common." He threw it into the bush. As I watched, it wriggled rapidly away through the undergrowth.

The river played a vital part in the life of Wailamepu: the children played and swam in it; the adults washed in it; the men caught fish from it, and everybody drank its water. Most important of all, it was the villagers' main highway that led to other settlements and to fresh hunting and fishing grounds. Men, women and children were all therefore expert boatmen and the landing was always crowded with canoes, some floating moored to posts, others submerged lest the blazing sun should crack them.

There were two kinds of craft, the corial, or dug-out canoe, made from a single log, and the aptly-named woodskin, a simple shell of bark.

We asked Clarence if we could see a woodskin being made.

"Is not easy," he said. "We only make woodskin from one tree, the purple-heart." (He pronounced it "pupple-heart"). "There no many in the bush, but I ask if any man know one."

He returned a few minutes later with an elderly man in a loincloth. Unlike Clarence's, his hair was not parted but cut in a fringe across his forehead. He was stouter than anyone we had so far met in the village, but he was impressively muscled.

"This John William," explained Clarence. "He say he know pupple-heart and will make woodskin for you."

We set off later that day in a corial with Clarence, two other men, and John William carrying a large felling axe.

We slipped down-river keeping close to the bank for nearly two miles. John William grunted, lifted his arm and pointed at a nondescript spot on the bank a few yards ahead. To my eyes, it had nothing to distinguish it from any other part of the forest. We ran the bows of the corial into the bank and clambered out. As we pushed through the thick brush close by the river, we entered the dim, almost ghostly atmosphere of the high forest, where our feet made little noise on the springy carpet of rotting leaves, and giant, branchless tree-trunks rose high on either side of us, like pillars in a Gothic cathedral, before they burgeoned out to form a canopy a hundred feet above.

At last we reached the purple-heart. John William silently took out his bush-knife and began felling the smaller saplings that surrounded its base. He stripped them of their spindly twigs and leaves and, using liana to bind them together, built a flimsy scaffold about five feet high around the bole of the selected tree. In this way he avoided having to cut through the wide base of the purple-heart which fanned out into radiating sheet-like buttresses.

He climbed on to the scaffold, and gripping the thin poles with his bare feet began the task of felling the tree. He worked steadily without pause and without saying a word. The shining axe flashed rhythmically and his dark skin glistened with sweat. Within five minutes he had cut through the white outer wood and had exposed the dark purple core which gives the tree its name.

The axe swung steadily until the tree gave an ominous creak. Composedly, John William climbed down from the scaffold and leaned on his axe. The enormous tree wavered and slowly hinged over. With gathering momentum it smashed through the forest, demolishing several of its smaller neighbours and, with a final thunderous crash, fell prone. The sunshine flooded through the gash it had torn in the forest canopy and for several minutes a hailstorm of leaves fluttered down.

Charles heaved a sigh of relief. "Praise be! At last some light to film by."

John William stolidly walked forward and inspected

the trunk. He wanted a section some twenty feet long, of unvarying diameter and completely smooth, and taking three small sticks, he laid them across the fallen trunk, apparently as an aid to measurement. With his bush-knife he cut a ring to mark the limit of the bows and stern. Then he removed a narrow strip of bark along the length of the trunk. This he cut up into wedges with which to prise the rest of the bark from the tree. One by one he inserted them, the bark parting from the wood beneath with a hissing, sucking sound as he pushed them farther in. At first, the stripped wood, wet with sap, was pure white, but as it was exposed, it changed to a reddish brown, marking progress by bands of increasing darkness.

Clarence and the other boys assisted. At no time did John William ask for any help or give any instruction. As we discovered, no Indian orders another to do anything. If your companions wish to help, then they will. If one is lazy, no one scolds him; everyone else just works a little harder.

At last, the long, flexible wedges had penetrated right round the tree, and the bark shell was quite free. Everyone gathered round to assist in the most critical operation of all. John William grunted a signal and the slit tube of flexible bark was carefully opened wide and slipped off its wooden core.

The Indians placed it gently on the ground. All examined it closely. Perhaps the removal had strained it too much and had cracked it; maybe there were some minute knot-holes which would spoil it.

John William decided that all was well and with his bush-knife began trimming the bows and stern into their correct tapering shape. After half an hour, he seemed satisfied. Clarence stood at one end, John William at the other and together they lifted the canoe-to-be, placed it on their heads, and walked down to the river and the corial.

Back at the village, the bark was left in the sun to dry and harden, but it was not yet finished, for the bows and the stern, though neatly tapered, were still on the same level as the rest of the canoe. If it were placed in the river, water would flow in at either end; the bows and the stern therefore had to be raised.

First John William tackled the stern. On each side he cut a six-inch groove running vertically down from the gunwale, about three feet from the end. The sides of the groove were not symmetrical; that nearest the stern sloped very much more than the other, so that when John William forced the stern upwards, the sloping side of the groove slid beneath the inner edge of the other side, tearing away the inmost layer of the bark and making it double back upon itself. To keep it in this position, he threaded strips of liana through holes on either side of the groove and pulled them tight. He repeated the process at the base of the bows.

The woodskin lay drying and hardening in the sun for several more days. At last John William carried it down to the river and launched it; it floated lightly on the surface of the water, perfectly balanced.

He climbed in carefully and for the first time since we had met him permitted himself a slight suspicion of a smile.

"Good," he said, and paddled off across the river.

Sitting talking to Clarence in his hut, I noticed above us, resting across the rafters, a long blow-pipe. Clarence took it down and showed it to me. It was ten feet long and made of two parts; an outer casing of polished palm-wood and inside, fitting snugly, a smooth lining formed by a gigantic hollow reed. Twelve inches from the mouthpiece were two labba-teeth, fastened on either side of the pipe with bees' wax.

Seeing I was curious, Clarence suggested that I should try it, and he gave me a dart — a splinter of palm wood, nine inches long. It was feathered at one end by a twist of cotton fibres. The other end was sharpened to a needle point. Before a hunting expedition this would be dipped in lethal curare poison prepared from vines in the forest.

Clarence explained that the two labba teeth enable you to make sure that the blow-pipe is held in exactly the same way each time it is used. This is important, for a blow-pipe is seldom exactly true and unwarped, and unless you hold it in the same position each time, you will not know what allowances to make when you aim. I put the dart inside, lifted the pipe to my lips and sighted it upon a small patch of fungus the size of a penny on a tree-trunk some ten yards away. I gave a sharp puff and to my astonishment the dart suddenly appeared quivering in the centre of the fungus patch. It had travelled with such force that a full inch of it was buried in the tree.

Effective though it obviously was, I was surprised to find that the men of the village still used a blow-pipe in preference to the shot guns which they could buy from the trade store at Kamarang.

I asked Clarence why this was so.

"Well," he said simply, "a blow-pipe is sometimes better. Maybe you find many birds in the forest feeding on a tree. You take a gun to them. Bang! And maybe you kill one — perhaps two. But the rest, when they hear the big noise, they fly away. With blow-pipe, you make no noise at all. You kill one; he fall to the ground and his friends they go on eating. So you see, you get many in this way."

Late one evening, Carlton trotted into the village. As usual, he was naked except for his loincloth. Over his shoulder he carried a blow-pipe and in his hand he held a cloth bag.

"Dayveed — you want these t'ings?" he said shyly.

I opened the mouth of the bag, and peered cautiously inside. To my astonishment and delight I saw at the bottom, lying perfectly still, several tiny humming birds. I shut the bag quickly, and excitedly ran into our hut where we had a cage made from a wooden crate ready for any animal that might turn up. One by one I put the little birds inside. To our relief, they immediately took to flight, darted rapidly through the air, hovered and then jerkily reversed to settle on the thin perches with which the cage was fitted.

I turned to Carlton, who had followed me.

"How you catch um?" I asked.

"Blow-pipe — and these t'ings," he replied, handing me a dart. It was exactly the same as the one Clarence had shown me except that its sharp point had been tipped with a little round pellet of bees' wax.

I turned again to the humming birds. The light blow

from the blunted dart had obviously only stunned them temporarily and they were now busily flitting to and fro in the cage.

One of them was a particularly beautiful creature, not more than two inches long, which I recognized: before we left London, I had visited the British Museum and had been captivated by one of the most delicate and gorgeous of all the humming bird skins there. It was labelled *Lophornis ornatus*, the Tufted Coquette. What had been beautiful even as a stuffed bird was here a breathtaking spectacle of movement and exquisite colour. On top of its tiny head it flaunted a short crest of vertical topaz red feathers. Beneath its needle-thin beak shone an iridescent emerald gorget and fanning out on either cheek was a sheaf of topaz feathers flecked with spots of emerald.

I was both entranced and dismayed, for although I had hoped to see this bird more than any other, we had decided that Jack should concentrate on collecting humming birds at Kamarang and we had not brought any of the necessary feeding equipment with us to the village.

Humming birds live mainly on nectar from forest flowers. In captivity they will readily accept a solution of honey and water enriched with milk extracts. As they only feed on the wing, special bottles with a cork at the top and a tiny spout at the bottom are needed to enable them to sip this substitute nectar. We had none of these things with us.

By now, it was dark and the little birds would not feed even if we had been able to offer them anything. We squatted in our hammocks and prepared a solution of sugar hoping that it might provide them with enough sustenance. Laboriously we tried to improvise feeding bottles by boring holes in the base of a section of bamboo and inserting small spouts from the stem of another tree. The finished result seemed very crude and we went to bed rather despondently.

We were wakened in the middle of the night by a tremendous rain-storm. The roof of the church had great gaps in it and we leapt out of our hammock to shift all our equipment and the humming birds in their cage to a dry spot. For the remainder of the night I slept only fitfully as the rain dripped down around me and collected in puddles on the floor. My single blanket became clammier and clammier. In my mind I could hear Bill saying that the seasons were deranged; that the rains might well begin early and that once they started they might continue for days on end without any real let up.

In the morning, with the rain still drumming on the roof and pattering on the floorboards of the hut, we did our best to persuade the humming birds to feed from our improvised bottles. We had no success; our substitute equipment was altogether too crude and the sugar solution rapidly dripped out of the bottle before the birds had taken any. We knew that they had to feed several times a day and that without regular supplies they would quickly wilt and die, like flowers without water.

With a wrench, we made the decision to release them, but having done so a weight lifted from our minds as the fragile things flew off through the door of our hut straight to the forest.

I sat in the doorway of the hut and brooded while

Charles busied himself among the stores and equipment. Outside, I could see the village through squalls of rain, huddled forlorn and desolate under the dismal sky. If this was indeed the beginning of the rainy season, all our plans for filming in the Mazaruni Basin would have to be abandoned and all the trouble and expense of getting there would have been wasted. I thought miserably of how exultant Jack would have been to have seen the Tufted Coquette and the other humming birds we had just released, and of how foolish and short-sighted we had been not to bring any feeding bottles.

Charles joined me. "I've made a few discoveries that might amuse you," he said. "First, that packet of sugar you've just emptied into your tea was our last. Second, I can't find the tin-opener. Third, the air is so damp that there's a great patch of fungus growing on one of the lenses of my camera, and fourth, I can't change that lens because the mounting has seized up."

He looked pensively at the rain. "If there's fungus growing on the glass of a lens," he continued, "it must be sprouting like mustard and cress on the exposed film. Not that that matters," he added mournfully, "because it's probably melted in the heat anyway."

There was nothing for us to do but to wait until the rain stopped. I returned to my hammock. Dejectedly, I took out of my kit one of the few books we had brought with us — *The Golden Treasury*.

I read for a few minutes.

"Charles," I said, "have you ever felt that William Cowper, 1731–1800, had any particular message for you?"

Charles made a vulgar but dismal reply.
"You're wrong," I said, "listen:

> 'O Solitude! where are the charms
>   That sages have seen in thy face?
> Better dwell in the midst of alarms
>   Than reign in this *'orrible* place'."

CHAPTER
EIGHT

Spirits in the Night

The rain continued intermittently for the last three days of our stay in Wailamepu. Although there were short periods of watery sunshine, serious photography was impossible, and we spent our time talking with Clarence, swimming in the tepid river with Carlton and Goodridge, and watching the everyday life of the people. This was pleasant enough, but we were constantly nagged by the thought that precious time was passing and that there were still many interesting aspects of village life which we had not yet filmed.

On the seventh day of our stay, we packed up our gear in preparation for the return of the canoe. Clarence was helping us spread ground-sheets over our pile of equipment to shield it from the rain dripping through the roof, when he straightened up and said conversationally, "Kenneth arrives in half-hour." His confident statement mystified me and I asked him how he could be so sure.

"I hear engine," he said, amazed that I should have asked. I put my head out of the hut door and listened. I could hear nothing but the swish of the rain on the forest.

Fifteen minutes later both Charles and I decided we could just distinguish the faint noise of an outboard motor, and in half an hour, exactly as Clarence had predicted, the canoe rounded the bend of the river with Kenneth at the tiller, bare-headed in the rain.

We left our friends at Wailamepu with regret, tempered by the pleasant anticipation of the dry clothes that awaited us at Kamarang. When we arrived there, we found that Jack's week had, on the whole, been more profitable than ours, for he had assembled quite a large miscellaneous collection of animals. There were numerous parrots, several snakes, a young otter and several dozen humming birds feeding very happily from glass bottles, the lack of which had forced us to release our Tufted Coquette.

We discussed plans for the week that now remained before our plane was due to return to Imbaimadai to collect us. Jack's ribs were still extremely painful, and though he was able to wander slowly through the forest with his Indian helpers looking for animals, he did not feel that he could face the prospect of travelling for several hours hunched up in a canoe. He had hoped to make a tour of many of the Indian villages in the area, for, as we had discovered, the Akawaio are all inveterate pet-keepers and it was possible that in some village a few miles away there was a rare creature, already tame, which its owner might be willing to sell. Such animals would be particularly valuable to us, for although it is difficult enough to catch a wild creature, it is often even harder to persuade it to settle down satisfactorily in captivity. That problem would scarcely exist if the animal had already been tamed by the Indians.

We decided therefore that while Jack remained at Kamarang, Charles and I should set out again on another canoe journey with the object of visiting as many villages as possible. We asked Bill's advice.

"Why not travel up the Kukui?" he suggested. "That's fairly heavily populated, and most of the villages are unmissionized, so you might hear some Hallelujah chants. Take the smaller canoe, and when you return down the Kukui, carry on up the Mazaruni to Imbaimadai. We will go up in the big canoe with all the animals and meet you there."

We set off the next day with the intention of spending our first night at Kukuiking, the village at the mouth of the Kukui. King George and another Indian named Abel came with us. The small canoe was heavily loaded with food, hammocks, a new supply of film, several empty cages ready for any animals we might find, and a large stock of blue and white glass beads with which to buy them. The colour of these beads was important, as Bill had told us when we bought them at his store. In the upper Kamarang, the inhabitants were very fond of red and pink as well as blue beads for the manufacture of their bead-aprons and other personal ornaments. On the Kukui they were more conservative, and blue and white beads were the only acceptable currency.

We reached Kukuiking in the late afternoon. Like Wailamepu it was a collection of simple wooden thatched huts in a clearing in the forest. The inhabitants stood morose and silent on the bank as we disembarked. As cheerfully as we could, we explained why we had come and asked if anyone had any pets which they would be willing to exchange for beads. One or two bedraggled little birds in filthy wicker baskets were reluctantly produced, and the villagers continued to regard us very suspiciously. This was unexpected after the genial and cheerful people we had known at Wailamepu.

"These people not happy?" I asked.

"The head-man, he very ill," King George replied. "He lie in his hammock for many weeks now and the piaiman — the medicine-man — he going to piai and cure him to-night. So they not so happy here."

"How does he piai?" I asked.

"Well, in the middle of the night he call spirits down from the sky to come and make the head-man better."

"Will you ask the piaiman if he will speak with us?"

King George disappeared in the crowd and returned with a prosperous-looking man in his early thirties. Unlike the rest of the villagers, who were wearing either dirty European clothes or loincloths and blue bead aprons, the piaiman was dressed comparatively neatly in khaki shorts and a shirt.

He looked at us rather sulkily.

I explained that we had come to the village to make pictures and recordings to take back to our country and asked if we might visit his seance that night.

He grunted and nodded.

"Could we perhaps bring a small light to take photographs?" I asked. He looked up and said severely, "Any man who show light when spirits in the hut — he die!"

I passed over the subject quickly and picked up my

tape recorder. As I did so, I plugged in the microphone and switched it on.

"May I bring this thing, then?" I asked.

"What kind o' t'ing, that?" he said disparagingly.

"Listen," I replied, and wound back the tape.

"What kind o' t'ing, that?" repeated the small loud-speaker rather tinnily. The suspicious look on the piaiman's face dissolved into a grin.

"You fine t'ing," he replied, addressing the machine.

"You agree that I bring it to-night, so that it can learn the spirit songs?" I continued.

"Yes. I 'gree," said the piaiman amicably and he turned on his heel and walked away.

The crowd dispersed and King George led us through the village to a small empty hut on the edge of the clearing. We dumped our kit and slung our hammocks. As the sun set, I practised loading and unloading the tape-recorder with my eyes tightly shut. It was not as easy as I had imagined, and I was constantly getting lengths of tape entangled with the knobs and levers of the machine. Eventually I felt reasonably confident that I could change reels in total darkness, but as a safeguard, I decided to go to the seance smoking a cigarette so that, initially at least, I should be able to solve any unforeseen difficulties by the light of its glow.

Late that night, Charles and I picked our way in the darkness through the silent village. The pointed silhouettes of the huts jutted black against the cloudy moonless sky. We entered the big hut to find it crammed with people. A small wood fire burned in the centre of the floor, illuminating the brown faces and bodies of the men and women who were squatting round it. In the semi-darkness beyond, we could just distinguish the dim white under-bellies of occupied hammocks, one of which we knew contained the sick head-man. King George was sitting on the wooden floor close to where we stood. Next to him we recognized the piaiman, squatting on his haunches and naked to the waist. In his hands he held two large sprigs of leaves, and by his side stood a small calabash full of what we later discovered to be salted tobacco juice.

We sat down close by him. I carried a lighted cigarette in my hand as I had planned, but the piaiman spotted it immediately. "Is no good!" he said aggressively, so I meekly stubbed it out on the floor.

The piaiman gave an instruction in Akawaio; the fire was kicked out and someone hung a blanket over the door. The shadowy outlines of the people sitting round me disappeared into blackness. It was totally dark. I groped for the recorder in front of me and found the switch so that I should be ready to begin recording as soon as the seance began. I heard the piaiman clear his throat and gargle with the tobacco juice. Then the leaves began to rustle. The eerie noise grew louder and louder, like a drum roll, until at its loudest it resolved itself into a hypnotic rhythmic beating which filled the hut. The piaiman's voice rose above the noise of the leaves in a moaning chant.

King George, just behind me, whispered in my ear. "Is calling a *karawari* spirit to come. He shaped like rope and all other spirits climb down him." After ten minutes the invocation came to an end. There was silence, broken only by the heavy breathing of someone close to me.

A rustle sounded high in the roof and slowly descended, increasing in volume until it ended abruptly with a thump on the floor. A pause — a gargle — and then a quacking noise. A strained falsetto voice began singing. Presumably this was the *karawari*. The song continued for several minutes, when suddenly, the pitch darkness was stabbed by a spurt of flame from the dying embers of the fire. In its momentary light, I saw the piaiman, still close by me, his eyes shut and his face contorted, with beads of sweat lining his brow. The flame died almost immediately, but it had broken the tension and the chanting and rustling stopped abruptly. Two boys on my left chattered uneasily.

The leaf rustlings began again. "The fire frighten the *karawari*," muttered King George in explanation. "He no come again. Piaiman now try to get *kasa-mara* spirit. He look like man and he bring a rope ladder."

The chant continued and once again in the blackness we heard a rustle descending from the roof. Another gargle — and a loud announcement in Akawaio which was replied to in fairly tart terms by a little girl somewhere on our right.

"What do they say?" I asked King George into the darkness.

"*Kasa-mara* say he work hard," he whispered, "and that head-man must pay well; and the girl, she say 'He only pay if you make him better'."

The leaves were now thrashing wildly and seemed to travel nearer the head-man's hammock. Soon the voices of several villagers began to join in with the spirit song, and someone beat time with thumps on the floor, until the song ceased and the rustles rose and faded away in the roof.

Another spirit arrived — more gargles — more songs. I felt almost suffocated by the stifling heat and the stench of sweating bodies in the pitch darkness of the hut. Every few minutes I had to change the tape on my recorder, but many of the spirit songs seemed repetitive and I did not record them all. After about an hour and a half, our initial awe began to wear thin. Charles, sitting by me, whispered in my ear, "I wonder what would happen if you wound back the tape now and made the first spirit reappear!" I was disinclined to experiment.

The seance continued for yet another hour — spirit after spirit descended from the roof, sang its song over the head-man's hammock and departed. Most of them had sung in a ventriloquist's falsetto, but eventually a different spirit arrived chanting in a retching, gulping manner that was quite frightening to listen to. I heard King George's voice whispering "This *bush dai-dai*. He very strong spirit of strangled man who came from topside in the mountains."

The atmosphere became oppressively tense and charged with emotion. The piaiman, sitting a few feet away from me, was now quite feverish for, in the darkness, I could sense his position almost exactly from the heat of his body. The revolting maniacal chant continued for several minutes and then abruptly stopped. There was a tense silence and I waited a little apprehensively in the darkness for what would happen next. The seance had obviously reached its climax. Was there perhaps going to be a sacrifice?

Suddenly a hot sweaty hand gripped my arm. I swung round, startled, but I could see nothing in the blackness. A man's hair brushed against my face. I was sure it was the piaiman and it flashed through my mind that the nearest white men were Bill and Jack, forty miles away.

The piaiman spoke hoarsely in my ear. "All is finish. I go make water!"

The next morning we were visited by a deputation of villagers, led by the piaiman, now once again smart and smiling. He stepped up on to the bark floor of our hut, which was raised twelve inches above the ground, and sat down.

"I come to hear my spirits," he said.

The villagers crowded into the hut after him and sat down in a circle around the recording machine. There was not room for all who wished to hear this miracle, and an overflow audience stood in a semi-circle outside the door.

I connected the speaker to the recorder and began playing the tapes. The piaiman was delighted and as the music of the seance floated out into the sunlight it was greeted with gasps of approval, nudgings, hushings and occasional nervous giggles. As each spirit song ended, I stopped the machine and made notes as the piaiman told me the name of each spirit, its appearance and origin and its capabilities. Some were invested with fearsome powers; others were efficacious with only minor ailments. "Man!" said the piaiman in an ecstasy of approval of one song, "that very powerful — and good for curing a cough!"

In all, I had recorded nine of these spirit songs. The last few inches of the last tape ran out of the spool and I switched off the machine.

"Where the rest?" inquired the piaiman peevishly.

"I'm afraid this machine humbug bad in the dark," I explained, "and he no able learn all the songs."

"But you no get the most powerful ones," the piaiman said, looking petulantly at me. "You no get the *awa-ui* or the *watabiara* and they fine spirits."

I apologized again. The piaiman seemed slightly appeased.

"Would you wish to see the spirits?" he asked.

"Yes, very much," I replied, "but I thought that no man was allowed to see them and that they only came down into a hut during the night."

The piaiman smiled confidentially.

"During the day," he said, "they have different shape and I keep them buried in my hut. Wait. I fetch them."

He returned holding in his hand a screwed-up piece of paper. He sat down on the bark floor once again and carefully opened the paper. Inside were a number of small polished pebbles. One by one he handed them to me, explaining the identity of each. One was a chip of quartz, another a long stick-like concretion, and another had four odd projections on it which he explained were the arms and legs of the spirit.

"I keep them in secret place in my hut, because these very powerful spirits and if another piaiman get them, then he can use them to kill me. This one," he added gravely, "is very, very, bad one."

He handed me a nondescript little pebble. I examined it with care and reverence, and passed it on to Charles. Somehow, between the two of us, we fumbled and the pebble dropped on to the floor and disappeared down a crack between the bark floorboards.

"He my most powerful spirit!" wailed the piaiman in anguish.

"Don't you worry, we'll find him," I said hastily, scrambling to my feet. I threaded my way through the appalled spectators and, lying down, wriggled under the floor of the hut. The ground was very gravelly and, as far as I could see, was covered almost exclusively with pebbles exactly like the incarnate spirit.

Charles, kneeling down on the floor above me, stuck a twig through the crack down which the precious pebble had disappeared. I looked anxiously at the place beneath, but there seemed to be nothing to choose between any of the pebbles. I selected one at random and passed it up through the crack to Charles, who offered it to the piaiman.

"No good!" the piaiman ejaculated icily, throwing it to one side with disdain.

"Don't worry," I bellowed from beneath the floor, "I'll find him," and passed out two other candidates. These met with the same treatment. During the next ten minutes, we proffered several dozen small pebbles. At last he accepted one and grunted grudgingly, "This my spirit."

I wriggled back into the sunlight, very dishevelled

and covered in dust. The villagers seemed as relieved as we were that the spirit had finally been recovered, and as I sat there I wondered whether we really had returned the correct stone, or whether the piaiman had decided to accept an ordinary pebble lest the villagers should think that he had lost one of his most powerful weapons and therefore some of his prestige.

The piaiman carefully placed the pebble with the others in his screw of paper and walked back to his hut to re-bury them.

We left the village that afternoon to continue our journey up the Kukui. As far as we knew, the head-man's health did not improve.

CHAPTER
NINE

The Kukui

The succession of rainstorms that had so depressed us at Wailamepu had now passed, and we travelled up the Kukui in baking sunshine. King George leaned on the tiller of the outboard engine, while Abel, our other Indian, stood in the bows, bare to the waist with a paddle in his hand, watching for hidden snags in the river ahead. Occasionally he turned to warn King George of a submerged boulder or to point out the easiest route through a tangle of fallen logs. Charles and I, meanwhile, sprawled in the centre part of the canoe, surrounded by empty cages and equipment. There was little to do but watch for morpho butterflies to flap out of the forest or speculate whether a splash close to one of the banks ahead was caused by an otter or an alligator.

When we had first met King George several weeks earlier, we had been misled by his ferocious scowl into thinking that he was ill-tempered and surly, and he had not endeared himself to us by his irritating habit of demanding gifts. If Charles took out a packet of cigarettes, King George would hold out his hand and say peremptorily, "Thank you for cigreet", and then accept the gift not as a favour but as a right. This always led to a general distribution of cigarettes, which meant inevitably that we should be short by the end of our trip, for we had budgeted carefully and accurately in order that our loads of stores might be kept to a minimum. However, we realized after a few days that the Indians regarded most property as communal: if one man had something that his companions lacked, then it was only right that he should share it. If food were short, then we should split our tin of bully beef with everyone in the canoe and, if we wished it, the Indians, as their share of the bargain, would give us some of their cassava bread.

As we got to know King George better, we valued him as a charming and kindly companion. He was full of information about the river and knew it intimately. At first, however, we found it difficult to convey our exact meaning to one another, for though King George spoke a limited amount of pidgin English, his words did not necessarily mean the same thing to all of us. "An hour" to King George was plainly only an indeterminate period of time, for if we asked him how long it would take to walk from the river-bank to a village in the "back-dam", he nearly always replied, "Eh, man! 'Bout one hour!" The unit of an hour was never divided or multiplied and "one hour" turned out to be ten minutes on one occasion and two and a half hours on another. This, of course, was entirely our fault for asking the question "How long?" for there was little reason why our units of time should mean anything to King George.

It was slightly more satisfactory to inquire "How far?" The answer to this varied from "'E no far" (which probably meant an hour's journey) to "Man, 'e faaar, far 'way", which meant it would not be possible to reach the place that day. We soon learned, however, that the most accurate way of assessing distance was in "points". By a "point", King George meant a bend in the river, but to translate "nine points" into time required some knowledge of geography, for near its mouth the river was straight for distances of several miles, whereas on the upper head-waters it twisted sharply every few minutes.

King George was ever obliging and always endeavoured to do what we wanted, though this willingness sometimes had slightly unfortunate results.

"Do you think we could possibly reach that village to-night?" I once said to him, implying by my tone of voice, that I hoped very much that we could.

"Well, man," he replied, "I t'ink we *mus'* meet it to-night," and he smiled encouragingly.

We were still travelling up an uninhabited part of the river at sunset.

"King George," I said severely, "where dis village?"

"Eh! 'E faar, far 'way!"

"But you say we meet it to-night."

"Well, man, we tried, didn't we?" he said in an injured tone.

As we travelled up the Kukui, the river became littered with fallen trees. Some of them we were able to sail round as they lay only part-way across the river; others were so long that they spanned the banks like a bridge, and these we were able to slide beneath. Sometimes, however, we would come to a giant tree lying almost submerged, which we could not avoid. Then King George would drive the canoe at it with an open throttle and at the last moment, cut the engine, swing the propeller column up out of the water in case it should foul, and so force the canoe half-way over the obstacle. We then had to climb out and, balancing on the slippery log, with the current tugging at our feet, haul the boat the rest of the way across.

We stopped at small settlements every few miles to ask for animals. There was no place we visited which did not have its complement of tame parrots hopping along the eaves of the huts or waddling irascibly around the village with their wings clasped behind their backs. The Indians, like us, value them for their bright colour and their ability to mimic human speech, and often, as we arrived, the birds would shriek abuse at us in Akawaio.

Adult parrots are difficult both to catch and to tame, so the Indians take the young chicks from their nests in the forest and rear them by hand. At one village, a woman gave us a nestling which she had only just obtained. It was a most appealing little chick with wide brown eyes, an absurdly large beak and a few scruffy feathers poking their quills through its otherwise naked skin. I could not bring myself to refuse it, but if I were to keep the charming creature I should have to take lessons on how to feed it. The woman laughingly told me what to do.

First, I chewed some cassava bread. As it saw me doing so, the little bird became tremendously excited, flapped its stumpy featherless wings and jerked its head

119

up and down in its enthusiasm for the coming meal. I then put my face close to it, whereupon, without hesitation, it stuck its open beak between my lips. It was now up to me to thrust the chewed cassava bread down its throat with my tongue.

This seemed a disgustingly unhygienic way of feeding any creature, but the woman assured me that there was no other method of successfully rearing a parrot chick. Fortunately ours was quite old, and a week later it was able to eat soft banana by itself and relieve us of the responsibility of chewing cassava every three hours.

By the time we were nearing Pipilipai, the village at the head of the river, we had bartered beads for macaws, tanagers, monkeys and tortoises as well as several unusual and brightly coloured parrots. The most unexpected of our purchases was a half-grown peccary, the wild pig of South America. The villagers who owned him seemed quite glad to pass him on to us for a comparatively small quantity of blue and white beads. At the time, it did not occur to us to wonder why. We soon found out.

We had not expected to acquire such a large creature as a peccary and we had no cages big enough for him, but he was quite tame and we naïvely decided to give him a little rope collar and attach him to a cross-stay in the bows of the canoe. This, however, was more difficult than it would seem, for the peccary, roughly speaking, tapered from his shoulders down to his snout and it was soon apparent that no normal collar would stay on him for one moment. We therefore tethered him by tying a rope harness round his shoulders and fore-legs. This, we thought, would be enough to dissuade him from trampling over other things in the canoe. Houdini, as we very soon called him, did not share this view and no sooner were we on our way than he lifted his fore-legs, one at a time, and with ease slipped out of the harness and picked his way down the canoe to begin eating the pineapples we had brought for our supper. We were disinclined to stop and make other arrangements to secure him, for we had to reach Pipilipai that night and our engine, as King George expressed it, was "humbugging plenty", so for the next hour I did my best to restrain Houdini's explorations by clasping his bristly body in an affectionate embrace.

At last we reached Pipilipai. The village lay ten minutes' walk away from the river and was one of the most primitive settlements we had so far seen. All the men wore loincloths and the women bead aprons. Their few circular huts were ramshackle and carelessly built. Some lacked side-walls, and all were built directly on the dry sandy ground instead of having floorboards like the huts at Kukuiking. Here, as at every other village, King George seemed to have a number of relatives and our welcome was cordial. There were parrots here too, but in addition, we saw a large crested curassow strutting among the huts. It was a glossy, black turkey-like bird with a handsome top-knot of curly feathers and a bright yellow bill. We learned that he was destined for the cooking-pot, but the villagers found our blue beads irresistible and gladly bartered him for six handfuls.

There were no vacant huts in the village so, with King George and Abel, we slung our hammocks in a hut that was already occupied by a family of ten. While Charles prepared the evening meal, I fondled Houdini and treacherously tied a new and elaborate harness round his shoulders as I did so. I then tethered him to a post in the centre of the village, put a pineapple and some cassava bread at his feet and exhorted him to lie down and go to sleep.

The night was not a good one. King George had not seen his relatives for some considerable time and long after nightfall he was chattering away, exchanging gossip. At about midnight a child suddenly began screaming and refused to be placated. Then one of the men climbed out of his hammock and re-stoked the fire in the centre of the hut. At last I managed to get to sleep, but it seemed that no sooner had I shut my eyes than I was being shaken by the shoulder and King George was saying in my ear, "De hog! 'E loose."

"We'll catch him when it's light," I murmured, and turned over to go back to sleep. The child started howling again and the unmistakable stench of pig filtered up my nostrils. I opened my eyes and saw Houdini rubbing his back against a hut post. Obviously, no one would get any sleep until he was re-tethered, so I wearily swung my legs out of my hammock and called softly to Charles to come and help catch him.

For half an hour Houdini cantered in, out and round the hut while Charles and I, barefooted and half naked, chased after him. Finally, we collared him and re-tied him to his post. Houdini, apparently satisfied now that he had wakened the entire population of the village, gave a hollow chop with his jaws and settled down on the ground with a pineapple between his front legs. We returned to our hammocks to try and sleep through the last few hours that remained before daybreak.

The journey back down-river began well. We had constructed a large cage for the peccary from thin saplings bound together with strips of bark, and this was wedged in the bows of the boat. Houdini behaved perfectly for the first half-hour; the curassow, tethered by a piece of string round its ankle, perched peacefully on the tarpaulin covering our equipment; tortoises rambled about the bottom of the canoe, parrots and macaws screeched amicably in our ears, and the capuchin monkeys sat together in a large wooden cage, affectionately examining one another's fur. Charles and I lay back in the sun, staring into the blue, cloudless sky and watching the green branches of the trees slip past us.

But this did not last long, for soon we reached a difficult snag of logs. We climbed overboard, and with our heads down, began hauling the canoe over a submerged tree-trunk. This was the moment for which Houdini had been waiting. Unknown to us, he had broken the fastenings of two of the lower bars of his cage, and in an instant he had jumped out of the canoe. I leaped into the water after him, nearly upsetting the boat, and after swimming a few yards, managed to catch him by the scruff of his neck. He kicked and splashed and squealed at the top of his voice, but at last I got him back into the remnants of his cage. Charles began the repair work while I stripped off my dripping clothes and laid them out on the tarpaulin to dry. Houdini, however, had obviously enjoyed his swim and was determined to have another, so for the rest of the journey one of us had to sit by his cage, re-tying the bars as quickly as he loosened them.

In the late evening we arrived at Jawala, King George's own village, half a mile up the river from Kukuiking. There we spent the night, having secured Houdini to a specially long tether, and quartered the rest of the animals in a derelict hut.

The next day was our last before we had to return to Imbaimadai. Most of the inhabitants of the village had been out hunting for the past week, but King George told us that they would return that day and sing Hallelujah in thanksgiving.

We had heard a great deal about this extraordinary religion which is peculiar to this part of South America and which, as its name suggests, is derived from Christianity. At the end of the last century, a Macusi Indian from the savannahs visited a Christian mission. He returned to his tribe and then claimed to have visions during which he visited a great spirit called Papa, high in the sky. Papa had said that he required worship by praying and preaching and told the Indian to return to the Macusi people and spread the new religion which was to be called "Hallelujah". The new beliefs were also adopted by neighbouring tribes from the Macusi so that, by the beginning of this century it had spread to the Patamona, Atecuna and to the Akawaio — all Carib-speaking tribes and very similar to each other. The missionaries apparently did not realize the Christian foundation of the religion. Generally, they condemned the beliefs that they found as being pagan and they whole-heartedly opposed them. No doubt their opposition was intensified when, as happened several times, new Hallelujah prophets declared that Papa had also predicted that white men would soon visit the Indians preaching from books and offering contradictory versions of their own religion. To judge from the missionaries' fierce hostility, we thought it must retain many of the Indians' old pagan beliefs, and we wondered what to expect on the hunters' return — a slightly warped version of Christian worship or a barbaric ritual.

We asked King George if we might film the ceremony. He grunted an assent and we settled down to wait.

After lunch we saw, in the distance, a woodskin coming down the river. Thinking that it might be the first of the returning hunters, we strolled down to the landing to meet it.

The canoe moored, and we blinked in astonishment at the incredible figure who walked up the path towards us. We had expected a slim lithe Indian, clad only in a loincloth. Instead we saw a garish old man, wearing a pair of brilliant blue linen shorts, a shrieking sports shirt spangled with aggressive multi-coloured designs representing Trinidadian steel-bands, and a Tyrolean felt hat complete with a white plume. This extraordinary apparition gave us a toothless leer, and stuck his hands in his ultramarine trousers.

"Man say you wish see Hallelujah dance. Before I dance, how much dollar you pay?"

Before I could say anything, King George, who was standing with us, began indignantly shouting a reply in

Akawaio, gesticulating wildly with both arms. We had never seen King George so animated.

The old man took off his hat and twisted it nervously in his hand. King George advanced on him, still fulminating, while the old man retreated backwards to his boat. He climbed in hastily and paddled back down the river.

King George rejoined us, still panting. "Man!" he replied with great sincerity, "I told that *wu'thless* fellow that in this village we sing Hallelujah for the praise of God and that if he come to sing for money then that is not true Hallelujah and we don't want him at all."

In the middle of the afternoon, the hunting party returned. Slung over their backs in woven baskets they carried loads of smoked fish, plucked carcasses of birds and kipper-brown joints of smoked tapir flesh. One man had a gun over his shoulder, and the rest were armed with blow-pipes and bows and arrows. Quietly and without speaking to King George or anyone else in the village, they walked up to the main hut, the floor of which had been brushed and sprinkled with water in readiness for them. They carried their loads inside and stacked them around the centre pole. Still silent, they left the hut and walked fifty yards along the path towards the river. There, they formed up in a column three deep, and began chanting. With slow rhythmic steps, two forward and one back, they advanced in procession towards the hut. At the head of the column, three young men led the singing and every few minutes turned to face the rest of the dancers. Slowly they progressed up the path, lurching forward and stamping to emphasize the simple rhythm of their chant. As they entered the hut, the song and the rhythm changed and they linked arms and circled the pile of fish and meat in the centre. Occasionally, a woman from the village wandered into the hut, and attached herself to the end of the procession. Several times in the droning three-note chant I distinguished the words "Hallelujah" and "Papa". King George squatted on his heels, pensively fiddling with a stick in the dust. The chant ended rather inconclusively and the singers stood about looking abstractedly at the ceiling or examining the floor. Suddenly the men who had led the procession began singing again and everyone re-formed into a line facing inwards, each with his right hand on his neighbour's shoulder. After ten minutes, the singers knelt down and in unison, spoke a brief and solemn prayer. They got to their feet and the man with the gun walked over to King George, shook him by the hand and lit a cigarette. The Hallelujah service was over and, strange though it was, we were left with an impression of deep sincerity.

That night was to be our last in an Indian settlement. I was unable to sleep. Towards midnight, I climbed out of my hammock and walked slowly through the moonlit village. As I approached the big round house, I heard the noise of voices and saw the flicker of lights through chinks in the wooden walls. I paused by the door, and I heard King George's voice say, "If you wish to enter, Dayveed, you very welcome."

I stooped and walked inside. The hut was lit only by a large fire which illuminated the smoked roof beams and the beautiful curves of several dozen giant calabashes which were grouped on the floor. Men and women lay in hammocks, criss-crossing from beam to beam; others squatted on small wooden stools carved in the stylized form of a tortoise. Occasionally a woman, naked except for her bead lap, rose and walked gracefully across the hut, the firelight dappling her red shining body. King George reclined in his hammock, holding in his right hand a small mussel-like shell, its two halves tied together with a string passed through holes just above the hinge. Reflectively he felt his chin, until he discovered a bristle. Then he closed the rims of the shell firmly around the hair and plucked it out.

The air was filled with a low conversation in Akawaio. One man squatted by the enormous calabashes, stirring them with a long stick and pouring out the pink lumpy fluid they contained into a smaller calabash which was handed round to everyone in the hut. This drink, I knew, was cassiri, and I had read of the way in which it is supposed to be prepared. Its main constituent is boiled grated cassava, but added to it is sweet potato and cassava bread which has been assiduously chewed by the women of the village. This addition of spittle is supposed to aid in the fermentation of the drink.

Soon, the small calabash was circulating among the people sitting close by me, and at length it was put in my hands. I felt it would be exceedingly impolite to refuse it, but at the same time, I could not dismiss from my mind the method of its manufacture. I lifted it to my lips, and as I caught the acid smell of vomit that rose from it, my stomach heaved. I began drinking and realized that if I had to taste that initial sip again, I might well be unable to control myself, so with an effort, I held the calabash to my mouth until I had drained it. With relief, I handed back the empty bowl and smiled weakly.

King George leaned out of his hammock and grinned approvingly.

"Eh, you!" he called to the man in charge of the calabashes, "Dayveed like cassiri and gets big thirst. Give 'im some more."

I was immediately handed another brimming calabash. As quickly as possible, I poured it down my throat. On second acquaintance, I managed to discount the nauseating smell and decided that although cassiri was a bit gritty and lumpy, its actual bitter-sweet taste was not wholly unpleasant.

I sat listening to the conversation for another hour. It was a fascinating scene and I was tempted to run back to our own hut and fetch a flash camera. Somehow the thought was repugnant, it seemed an infringement of the hospitality which had been so generously offered to me by King George and his companions. Contentedly, I sat in the hut until the early morning.

Next day dawned fine. We loaded the canoe, put a protesting Houdini into a reconstructed and strengthened cage and with all the rest of the animals squealing and chattering around us, we sailed off down the river, past Kukuiking and into the wide Mazaruni. The weather began to worsen and soon light rain started to fall. Charles and I huddled under a groundsheet in an attempt to keep dry. Black clouds accumulated overhead and the drizzle changed suddenly to sheets of rain which hit our knees forcibly and painfully as we sat with the groundsheet over our heads.

At this moment, Houdini elected to make his final bid for a swim and was half-way over the side before I could catch him. In the few minutes that it took me to get him back into his cage, I was drenched and rainwater gushed down my neck and through my shirt. There seemed little point in returning to the doubtful shelter of the groundsheet, and I spent the rest of the journey sitting in the bows, forlorn and cold, forestalling Houdini's attempts at escape.

The rain stopped just before we reached Imbaimadai, but Jack met us with the devastating news that the storm had turned the airstrip into a sodden morass and that Bill was already calling Georgetown on the radiophone to cancel the plane.

Depressed, we carried everything up to the hut by the airstrip where we had stayed for our first night in the district. Bill greeted us with a note of guarded optimism. "If there is no more rain and a lot of sun, the strip *may* have dried out by to-morrow." We settled down to wait and hope.

Fortunately we had something to distract us, for Jack's menagerie had grown considerably since we had last seen it.

He had collected many new and beautiful birds, whose flamboyant names matched their good looks — Black Throated Cardinals, Yellow Crowned Troupials, Golden Hangnests and Graceful Mocking Birds. The most glorious of them, however, was a young male Cock of the Rock. He was about the size of a pigeon, and except for his black wings and tail he was dressed overall in brilliant orange feathers. On his head, tipping rakishly over his yellow beak, he flaunted a vertical semicircular flame-coloured crest rimmed with purple brown, which gave him the appearance of a tipsy dandy. Excitedly, we asked Jack where this wonderful bird had come from, for the Cock of the Rock is famed for its spectacular courtship dance in which several dozen of these splendid males perch in trees around a small circular dancing ground and one at a time, in turn, flutter down to strut and dance until almost exhausted. Few people have ever seen this performance, and the presence of Jack's specimen must mean that the dances took place somewhere nearby.

Jack told us that the bird had been brought to him from the Upper Kamarang River by an old Indian named Benjie, who had said that he knew where the Cock was dancing at this very moment.

Bill joined in the conversation. "If this airstrip doesn't dry out," he said, "the only way you chaps will be able to get back to Georgetown is to charter an amphibian plane to land on the river at Kamarang. It may be some days before Georgetown has one available, so you're probably going to have plenty of time to see if old Benjie is speaking the truth."

Within half an hour it was raining heavily once again and we concentrated our thoughts on the Cock of the Rock to console us for the delay and waste of time the rains were causing us.

All that day we sat at Imbaimadai waiting for a few hours of baking sun to make the airstrip serviceable again. The sun shone, but only spasmodically. There was nothing to do but lie in our hammocks and be patient.

On the second day we discovered a novel form of entertainment to pass away the time. Charles had complained of a painful itch in the sole of his foot. Bill diagnosed it immediately.

"Probably a jigger flea," he said. "Have you been walking barefoot in a sandy village?" We told him of our midnight chase after Houdini in Pipilipai.

"Well that's where you got infected, no doubt," Bill replied. "These little fleas infest the sand of a village and if a female gets the chance she bores into your flesh and then begins producing eggs inside herself until she swells to the size of a pea. You'd better get King George to pick it out for you. He'll do it much better than you or I can, and it's rather important not to burst the thing or else all the eggs may re-infect you."

Charles lay in his hammock looking at the roof while King George went to work on his naked foot with a pin.

"Eh man! you get plenty," he said exultantly. "'E sweet itch?" Charles gave him an acid look.

At the end of an hour King George had excavated twenty-seven little pits and removed twenty-seven jiggers. As I sat watching, the soles of my feet began to itch too and when King George had finished he started work on me. To Charles's scorn I could only provide eight.

On the third day a particularly violent storm sealed

the fate of the airstrip. We went outside with Bill and dug our heels into the waterlogged ground. "No plane is going to be able to land here for the next three months," he said. "The rains have really started."

That afternoon he radioed Georgetown, declared Imbaimadai closed to planes for the season and asked that an amphibian should come to Kamarang to pick us up. The message came back that one would be free for charter in four days' time.

The following day we set off on the return to Kamarang. With the onset of the rainy season the river was transformed. The water had risen ten feet and, sucking and gurgling, slid between the branches of trees on the banks. Many of the landmarks with which we were familiar — boulders, sandbanks and clearings — were submerged beneath the turbid opaque flood water. The trees themselves were also changed, for many of them had suddenly put out new leaves which varied in colour from a silver ashen yellow to a deep russet. The sun shone irritatingly and we wondered if we had been patient enough at Imbaimadai.

That night at Kamarang we met Benjie, the Cock of the Rock collector, a little wizened man with a wrinkled brown face and puckered eyes. He spoke quickly in a high-pitched voice.

"Yes, I able show you place where Cock dance. I take you to-morrow."

We now had two clear days left before our plane was due. To reach Benjie's village would involve a full day's travel up the Kamarang, but as we should have the current of the flooded river to help us on our way back, we should have just enough time to visit the dancing ground early in the morning of the second day before we had to return. But even if we managed to find the place, there seemed very little chance that the birds would be performing in the few hours that we should be there. Nevertheless, we decided that even such a remote possibility should be grasped. It would never come again.

We reached Benjie's village late the next night and as we ate our meal he told us that the dancing ground was very close.

"Dance to-morrow, plenty early," he said optimistically, "if no rain."

We rose before dawn. To our dismay it was already drizzling and as we threaded our way through a thicket of tall white ground orchids at the back of the village, we had little hope of seeing anything of the bird. After half an hour's walk through thicker bush Benjie stopped. The forest floor had hitherto been covered in rotting leaves and fallen branches, but at Benjie's feet was a circular patch of bare polished earth two feet in diameter.

"Dis where Cock dance, plenty time," Benjie whispered. He picked up a fragment of twig lying in the middle of the patch and showed it to us. "Cock always keep ground very clean; this thing say they not come for some days. It rain too much."

We sat on a fallen rotting log ten yards away from the dancing ground.

"I try call one," Benjie whispered. He screwed up his face, lifted his head and gave a loud two-note falsetto squawk. We sat in silence. The rain dripped gently through the tiers of leaves of the forest, and the moisture-laden atmosphere condensed and trickled down our faces and clothes.

Benjie called again.

Suddenly, we saw a glint of colour far off in the gloom of the forest and heard an answering call. Benjie cupped his hands round his mouth and replied.

Cautiously the bird came nearer, flitting from tree to tree, each flight an explosion of colour. Soon the glorious orange bird was within fifteen yards of us. It cocked its head to one side so that we saw its piercing red eye and its wonderful crest in profile. It hopped from branch to branch, as though baffled, for nearly two minutes while we held our breath in jubilation at seeing this rare and exquisitely lovely creature. Then it was gone.

"Is no good," said Benjie. "Is too wet. He no dance."

We had already stayed later than we had intended and if we were not to miss the plane we would have to start back immediately. Regretfully, we picked up the cameras and walked back through the dripping forest.

The next day, the little amphibian plane came down on the Kamarang River exactly as arranged. As we flew east, we looked beneath us at the forest now no longer basking in the sun but smoking with trails of wispy cloud. All around the aircraft were stacked cages of birds and wriggling bags of snakes. At my feet lay a long airtight wooden box. Fitting tightly inside it were three sealed biscuit tins, and inside the tins, together with desiccants to absorb the moisture, were packed five thousand feet of exposed film.

Within an hour and a half of saying good-bye to Bill and Daphne Seggar, we were once again walking along a tarmac road between the modern ferro-concrete buildings of Georgetown.

CHAPTER
TEN

Shanties and Snakes

Georgetown seemed particularly attractive to us when we returned from the Mazaruni. We relished the thought of eating meals which were not emptied straight from tins and which we had not cooked ourselves, and of lying flat on a bed covered with clean white sheets instead of curling in a hammock under a damp crumpled blanket excavated from the bottom of a musty kit-bag. But we also had a great deal of work to do: fresh supplies of food had to be bought and plans for the next trip to be made; the exposed film had to be sorted, repacked and sealed, and taken down to the city's cold store to be deposited in a refrigerated vault. The animals had to be transferred to the larger, permanent cages which Tim Vinall had had built in readiness for them, and some of them had to be taken to the Georgetown Zoo, which was already looking after the anteater and was now offering to take Houdini and the crested curassow as temporary lodgers.

To make the best use of the cages at his disposal, Tim decided to shift some of the Rupununi animals into different quarters. Chiquita, the capuchin monkey that Teddy Melville had given us, was the last to be moved.

137

Tim opened the door of her cage and took her out. She cuddled sentimentally in his arms. As he opened the door of her new cage, she gave him a deep bite in the ball of his thumb, skipped out of his arms and gambolled across the lawns of the Botanic Gardens. We all set off in pursuit, Tim sucking his bleeding hand. Chiquita was well ahead, so she stopped and scratched herself until we had almost caught up with her. Then she ran up the trunk of a large tree which stood on the edge of the gardens, overhanging the road outside. Rather pointlessly, I laboriously climbed after her. It was not until I was half-way up that I noticed that she had selected a tree which bore one of the largest hornets' nests that I have ever seen. As she ran along the branch from which it hung, the insects poured from their nest and encircled my head in an angry cloud. The monkey stopped at the far end of the branch and looked round coyly. I retreated hastily with the insects buzzing around me, and ruefully ran out of the gardens to join Charles and Tim in the road outside. Chiquita looked down from above and gibbered at us. The game could now go no farther; we were in the road, she in the tree. There was no fun in this, so she leaped into the branches of another tree on the opposite side of the road, nimbly scrambled down to the ground and set off down the busy street. Once more we careered after her.

The road was thronged with cyclists who stopped in amazement as the little monkey scampered past them pursued by three puffing Englishmen. As I ran, it occurred to me that the only way of catching her without being bitten was to throw a cloth over her and bundle her up. Although I had not got a cloth, I did have a shirt, and as the cyclists shrieked with laughter and yelled encouragement, I stripped it off as I went. At last, half-naked, I caught up with her and dropped my shirt over her head. She tripped up in its folds and I stooped and quickly gathered her into my arms. Chiquita stuck her head out of the shirt and looked apologetic. Now that the game was over, she was prepared to be sweetness itself, but I was taking no chances and carried her all the way back to the Gardens swathed in my shirt to put her into her new cage.

Our next journey should have been to a remote area on the edge of the Amazon basin in the far south. There two missionaries were living and working with a very primitive and interesting Amerindian tribe. The only way for us to reach them, apart from a march through the forest which, there and back, would take six weeks, was to land in an amphibian plane at a point on a river some fifty miles away from the tribe, having previously arranged with the missionaries by radio that canoes and porters would be there to meet us. This was our plan, but to our dismay we discovered that the missionaries had been out of radio-contact with Georgetown for the past three weeks. Their wireless must have broken down, and so there was no way of warning them of our arrival. To land without advance preparations would be to maroon ourselves in uninhabited forest without guides, porters or any means of transport.

An alternative scheme, however, was already forming in our minds. We had been left a message by the manager of a mining company to say that the forest round one of his exploratory camps at Arakaka in the northern part of the colony was particularly rich in animals and that at the camp itself there were several tame creatures which he would willingly give us.

We looked at the map. Arakaka lay at the head of the Barima River which ran roughly parallel to the northern boundary of Guyana and then swung north-west to empty into the estuary of the Orinoco. The map told us two other important facts. First, a small red symbol of an aeroplane, printed by the name "Mount Everard" fifty miles down-river from Arakaka, showed us that we could reach that point at least by amphibian plane. Second, a cluster of red circles along the southern bank of the Barima indicated that there were many small gold workings; from this we inferred that there must be considerable traffic along the river and that there was therefore every chance of finding a boat which could take us up from Mount Everard to Arakaka.

We investigated further. The Airways told us that the only time during the next fortnight that the amphibian was free for charter was the following day, and the Docks told us that in twelve days' time a passenger ship would be returning to Georgetown from Morawhanna, a small settlement near the mouth of the Barima. If we were to go, we should have to go to-morrow. Unfortunately there was no means of warning the mining manager, for his only contact with his office in Georgetown was by radiophone, and while he could call his office, his office could not call him. We therefore left a message to be passed on the next time he called, saying that we would be arriving in Arakaka in three or four days' time. We booked passages for our return on the ship, s.s. *Tarpon*, and we chartered the amphibian.

The next day, we were in the air en route for Mount Everard, wondering whether these rather hurried and impromptu preparations would get us to Arakaka and back again to Georgetown within a reasonable time. After an hour's flying, the pilot yelled at us over his shoulder. "That," he screamed above the roar of the engine, "is the best they can do for a 'mount' hereabouts!" and he pointed below to a small hump rising about fifty feet above the forest of the flat coastal plain. Just beyond it flowed the Barima River, and at its foot clustered a few small houses, the first we had seen for seventy miles.

The pilot put the plane into a steep bank and shaped up for a landing on the river.

"I sure hope there's someone down there," he bellowed, "because if there ain't, there will be no one to moor the plane and no canoe to get you ashore, so we'll just have to take off again and go back the way we've come."

"A fine time to tell us that!" muttered Charles.

The plane touched the surface of the river with a shudder, and through the spray spurting on the windows we saw to our relief a group of men standing on the jetty. At least we were going to be able to disembark. The pilot shut off the engines and shouted to the men to bring canoes. We unloaded all our gear and paddled over to the jetty. The plane took off with a roar, wished us luck with a tilt of its wings and disappeared.

The settlement at Mount Everard consisted only of six shacks grouped round a sawmill on the jetty. Hauled in the slipway close by lay a pile of huge, mud-blackened tree-trunks that had been felled higher up-river and floated down to the mill. The jetty itself was covered in cones of fragrant salmon-coloured sawdust. The foreman of the mill, an East Indian, showed no sign of surprise at our unheralded descent from the skies, but simply and politely showed us to an empty hut where we could spend the night. We thanked him gratefully and asked him if there was any boat that might be going up-river towards Arakaka in the morning. He removed his peaked baseball cap and scratched his oily black hair.

"No," he said, "I not think so. The only boat here is the *Berlin Grand*." He pointed to a large single-masted wooden vessel lying with her sails furled by the jetty. "She leave to-morrow with timber for Georgetown. But maybe something pass in two — three days."

We settled down in our hut and prepared ourselves for a long stay. After supper, in the dusk we walked down to the river. As we approached the *Berlin Grand*, we were hailed by the skipper, a hefty, elderly African dressed in an oily, torn shirt and trousers, who was lying on the deck with his back against the mast. At his invitation, we went on board and met the other three members of the crew, all Africans, who were sitting with him enjoying the cool of the evening. We joined them and explained what we were doing on the Barima; they in turn told us about their life shipping sawn planks to Georgetown and bringing back stores for the mill.

"Do you know many of the old sea-songs?" I asked.

"Shanties? Yes, man, Ah knows plenty," the skipper

said. "'Fact my singin' name is Lord Lucifer — dat's de man-devil. Ah have dat name because when Ah gets some o' de right spirit inside me, Ah becomes a fiend to myself — a devilish man. An' de fus' mate, he know even more song than Ah do, 'cause he walk in dis bush even longer dan me. His name, de Great Smasher. You want to hear shanty?"

I said that we would like to hear some very much and that we would also like to record them. Lord Lucifer and the Great Smasher held a muttered conference and then turned to me.

"O.K. chief," Lord Lucifer said. "We sing. But you know, chief, Ah cain't remember de *good* songs 'ceptin' dere's a big supply o' lubrication. You get dollar?"

I produced two.

Lord Lucifer took them with a polite smile and called one of his crew.

"Present dese," he said solemnly, "to Mistah Kahn at de sawmill, wid de compliments o' de *Berlin Gran'* an' insinuate" — his voice dropped to a whisper — "dat we require a supply o' R-U-M."

He gave me a wide toothless smile.

"Wid a little bit o' high spirit inside me, I'se a powerful singer."

While the lubrication was being obtained, I set up the recorder. Five minutes later, the deck-hand reappeared with sad news.

"Mistah Kahn," he said, "gets no more rum."

Lord Lucifer emitted a heavy sigh and rolled his eyes.

"We'se gwine to have to work on a substitoot fuel,"

he said. "Request Mistah Kahn to supply two dollars wu'th o' Ruby Wine."

When the messenger returned, he was clutching a vast number of bottles which he set down in ranks on the deck.

The Great Smasher picked one up and looked at it with distaste. In the centre of its garish label was a violently coloured design representing, rather inappropriately, a pile of lemons, oranges and pineapples. Above, printed in red capitals were the words "RUBY WINE" and beneath, more discreetly in small black letters, "Port-type".

"I'se 'fraid we'se goin' to need plenty o' dis stuff before we gits started really well on de good songs," he said apologetically.

He pulled the cork, passed the bottle to Lord Lucifer, took one himself, and with a martyred air, manfully set about the task of lubrication.

Lord Lucifer wiped his mouth on the back of his hand and cleared his throat.

"I'se shoutin' since de time I'm small,
I never like de t'ing dey call work at all.
Look me gran'fader dead, goin' to work
Look me gran'mudder dead, comin' from work
And me uncle, look 'e dead, working on a truck
So I don' see who de *hell* will get me to work."

We applauded.

"Ah know better ones dan dat, chief," he said modestly, "but Ah cain't remember dem jus' yet."

He opened another bottle. Better ones soon began

to arrive. The tunes of many of them I recognized as having been published in a collection of West Indian folk-songs. The printed words had seemed a little effete and lacking in coherent theme. Lord Lucifer's versions, however, differed considerably. Quite obviously, they were the originals from which the published ones had been derived, but they were so appallingly bawdy that as they rang out over the river, I was lost in admiration for the ingenuity of the folk-song collector who had managed to twist and trim the lyrics so that they became printable.

As the evening wore on and darkness fell, a chorus of frogs provided a honking accompaniment. The deck-hand was despatched for further supplies of lubrication. We learned what happened when "Moskeeta married san' fly's daughter", and also of the no doubt apocryphal doings of Tiny McTurk's father in a shanty which began, "Michael McTurk was a river navigator, and a great bush governor."

The supply of Ruby Wine was dwindling but no further lubrication seemed to be necessary. Lord Lucifer and the Great Smasher were now singing in unison.

"Madre, I'm tired of you, ah-ha.
Jus' because, you not really true, ah-ha.
For every time I walk down de stran'
I hear you in love, look, with some Yankee man
I'm going to beat you, he was a big Yankee man
I'm goin' to kick you, he was a black Yankee man
I'm goin' to fight you, he was a rough Yankee
    man."

The variants on this last line seemed endless and as they sang them, the two singers began to compete to see who could provide the best version.

"I'm goin' to crack you, he was a tall Yankee man," sang the Smasher.

We got to our feet and explained we must go.

"Good night, chief," said Lord Lucifer genially. "I'm goin' to flog you, he was a huge Yankee man."

We picked our way in the darkness down the gang-plank and walked up towards our hut.

The Great Smasher's voice lifted in triumph, and floating through the night came his masterpiece.

"I'm goin' to *exterminate* you, he was a *vast* Yankee man."

Lord Lucifer's reply was lost among the honkings of the frogs.

Next morning, the wharf was empty; the *Berlin Grand* had sailed at daybreak for Georgetown with a cargo of crab-wood, mora and purple-heart. The settlement seemed deserted, the sawmill silent, sweltering in the moist oppressive heat. We walked up the mount with nets in our hand to see if we could find any animals. Little stirred in the broiling sun. A huge nest of leaf-cutting ants sprawled over the side of the hill, embracing its slope in a net-work of tracks; but no ants were to be seen. Occasionally, our attention was drawn by a rustle in the grass and we caught a brief glimpse of a lizard's tail. A few butterflies flew lazily and jerkily in front of us. Apart from these and the whirrs of crickets, there was no sign of life. If we were to be marooned at Mount

Everard for long, it was clear that we should have to trek much farther into the forest away from the sawmill to find any animals.

Late in the afternoon, the brooding quietness was broken by the distant roar of an engine. Thinking it might be a launch, we ran down to the wharf to see if there was any chance of it taking us farther up-river towards Arakaka. The roar increased until round the bend at enormous speed came a tiny dugout canoe. It swept round in a wide flamboyant arc, casting a spectacular bow-wave. As it straightened out, the engine was cut off and the boat slid neatly up to the wharf. Two smart East Indian boys climbed out wearing singlets and shorts and white cloth peakless caps.

We introduced ourselves.

"Me, Ali," said one, in reply. "Him — Lal."

"We wish to meet Arakaka," Jack said. "You able carry us?"

Ali, who was the spokesman of the pair, explained volubly that they were travelling up river to cut wood, but that they were not going as far as Arakaka, that an extra load would not only slow them down but also increase the chance of sinking to danger-point, and that anyway, they had not got nearly enough fuel to get to Arakaka and that even if they had, they would not have enough to get back. Clearly, it was impossible.

"But," said Ali hastily, "if you get plenty dollar, maybe we go."

Jack shook his head and pointed out that the boat was exceedingly small, that it was uncovered and that we could not therefore protect our equipment from ruin by rain and that, now he came to think of it, we did not really want to reach Arakaka either.

Ali and Lal were delighted by this and we all sat down on the piles of sawdust on the wharf to savour to the full every move in this elaborate game of bargaining. At length, Ali agreed that, although he would undoubtedly lose a great deal of money on the deal, he would take us up to Arakaka the next morning for the paltry sum of twenty dollars.

That night there was a tremendous storm. The rain beat on the roof of our hut and cascaded through holes in the thatch on to the floor. Charles, having got up to make sure that the equipment was in a dry place, decided that as the noise of the storm would prevent him from sleeping anyway, he would seal everything in plastic bags in case a similar downpour caught us unprotected in the open canoe the next day.

In the morning, it seemed that we could not make the journey anyway, for Ali's canoe had filled with rain during the night and had sunk. It now lay on the bottom of the river with its engine under four feet of water.

Ali and Lal, however, were not at all put out, and had already begun salvage operations. With difficulty, they dragged the bows up on the bank. Lal began baling out water while Ali fished up the engine and hauled it ashore, water pouring from all its parts.

"Is all right," he said. "We get him to go soon."

Nonchalantly, they began to dismantle it. Charles, who has a considerable knowledge of mechanical things, was doubtful. "Don't you realize," he said, "that the coil is soaking wet? The engine will never start until it is completely dry."

"Is all right," Ali said again, unmoved. "We cook 'um," and taking off the dripping coil, he carried it over to a fire and put it on a bent plate of glowing metal. Then he removed the plugs from the engine and together with other pieces of the mechanism, soaked them in petrol and set them alight. Every other removable piece of the engine was unscrewed and laid out on Lal's singlet to dry in the sun. This process seemed to have a horrid fascination for Charles, who sat watching and occasionally offering to help in what was obviously, to him, a completely new approach to mechanical repairs.

Within two hours, the engine was re-assembled. With a flourish, Ali pulled the starting cord and to our astonishment the engine roared into life. Ali stopped it. "We ready now," he said.

Our misgivings over the size of the canoe were fully justified, for when we had loaded it with all our belongings and climbed in ourselves, there was barely an inch of free-board, and the slightest movement by any one of us was sufficient to make the river water pour over the side. Our journey that day was therefore a little uncomfortable for we were very cramped and the enforced rigidity of our positions became extremely painful after a few hours. Nevertheless, we were very happy; we were on our way to Arakaka.

Even as we travelled, we saw more signs of animal life than we had ever done in the Mazaruni Basin. Morpho butterflies were very common and twice we saw snakes swimming in the river close by us; but we could do no more than slightly incline our heads to look at them for fear of capsizing the canoe. Occasionally we passed little clearings in the forest on the banks, with three or four half-naked Africans or East Indians standing watching us as we passed. Beneath them in the river lay logs which they had felled in the forest and tied together into rafts, ready to be floated down to the saw-mill. Ali and Lal called out greetings and we slowly and noisily crawled past them. Once a small battered launch swept by us at speed and we spent an anxious few minutes baling hard to prevent our canoe from being totally swamped as we bobbed up and down in its wake.

Late in the afternoon we arrived at a small village. It looked pleasant and prosperous. Plots of cassava and pineapples had been laid out among the lush grass of the river-bank and tall slender coconut palms grew between the solidly built huts. The Amerindian inhabitants, dressed in dirty European clothes, lined the banks watching us. Behind them and dwarfing them, stood two tall Africans.

We moored and climbed out; after five hours' travel, we were grateful for the chance to stretch our legs and move freely again.

Ali began unloading the canoe.

"This village Koriabo," he said. "Arakaka another five hours topside. We no take you farther. I t'ink canoe, 'e sink if we go again, and in this village, man gets launch. He take you Arakaka. Here — twenty dollar," and to our surprise he produced the notes and offered them to us. "No," said Jack, "you bring us halfway — you keep ten dollar."

Ali flashed a smile. "Thank you," he said, "now we go cut tree," and with Lal in the bows, he pushed the canoe out from the bank. The tiny boat, freed of its enormous load, once more surged speedily along the river and disappeared round the bend.

The taller of the two Africans walked up to us.

"My name, Brinsley McLeod," he said. "I get launch and take you Arakaka for ten dollar. It go down to Mount Everard to get fuel dis morning — maybe you see um — but it come back to-morrow and den I take you." We gladly accepted his offer and walked up to the hut that had been allocated to us, well content at the thought of travelling the next day in the powerful and roomy boat that had swept by us earlier in the afternoon.

The next morning, as we were finishing breakfast, the other African paid us a visit. He was considerably older than McLeod. His face was scarred and deeply lined, and his eyes, the whites blood-shot and yellowing, had a slightly crazed wild look about them.

"Brinsley no say de truth," he said darkly. "Dat boat no come back to-day, nor to-morrow, nor de nex' day. De men dey stay in Mount Everard drinkin' rum. Why you want to go Arakaka?"

We told him that we were collecting animals.

"Man," he said gloomily, "dere's no cause to go Arakaka for varmints like dat. I get plenty o' dem t'ings on my gold claim in de bush here. Dere's camoodie, alligator, labaria snake, antelope, numb-fish. Aall dem t'ings, plenty. Dey no use to me, you can take um, 'cause dey humbug me bad. Dey *pests*."

"Numb fish?" asked Jack. "You mean electric eels?"

"Yes, plenty," he said, heatedly. "Small ones, big ones, some o' dem bigger dan a canoe. Dey powerful bad varmints; dey kin *shack* you t'ru de boat, 'ceptin' you wear de rubber long boots. One time dey shack me and t'row me on de groun' an' Ah lies dere in de boat all dizzy in de head for t'ree days 'fore I able get up. Yes *sah*, I get all dem t'ings on my claim, an' I take you dere if you want to see um."

We finished breakfast hastily and walked down with him to his canoe. As we paddled up river, he told us more about himself. His name was Cetas Kingston and he had been prospecting for gold and diamonds in the forests of Guyana all his life. Sometimes he had made a strike but always the money had disappeared quickly afterwards, leaving him as poor as ever. A few years ago he had discovered the claim he was taking us to now. This, he said, was the really good one, the one which would make him a rich man in a few years and enable him to give up working in the bush and settle down in comfort on the coast.

We turned off the main river into a side creek and soon we came to a post stuck in the swampy bank. A rectangular piece of tin, nailed on top, bore the crudely painted words "Name of Claim HELL. Claimant C. Kingston", and beneath it a licence number and a date.

We climbed out of the canoe and followed Cetas along a narrow track into the bush. After ten minutes we stepped from the gloom of the forest into a sunlit area where the trees had been felled and the incomplete frame-work of a large hut had been built.

Cetas turned round to us, his eyes blazing. "Aall roun'

dis place," he said, sweeping his arm in a circle, "dere's gold in de groun'. An' it's none o' dis no-good nugget gold. You fin' one of dose t'ings one day an' den nut'ing for five year. No *sah*! In dis groun', four feet down you come to de red gold-dirt, redder dan blood. Dat's de true gold, an' all I got to do is to dig it out. Look, I show you."

He seized the long-handled spade he had brought with him and frenziedly began to dig a small pit. Muttering to himself he hurled the spade into the ground. Sweat dripped off his black, tired face and soaked his shirt. At last he threw down the spade and groped in the bottom of the hole. He brought up a handful of rust-coloured gravel.

"Dere, you see," he said hoarsely. "Redder dan blood." He poked it with his forefinger and rambled on, almost ignoring us.

"'Course, I'se old man, but I get two sons an' dey fine boys. Dey ain't gwine to learn no trade. Dey'se gwine to come here and dig. An' we'll plant cassava an' pineapple an' lime aroun' de shack an' we'll bring in labour an' den we'll dig all dis dirt up an' wash out aall de gold."

He stopped talking, threw the gravel in his hand back into the hole and got to his feet.

"I t'ink we go back Koriabo," he said dejectedly, and walked down the trail to the canoe. He seemed to have forgotten that he had brought us to his claim to show us animals and to be obsessed with the sudden fear that though gold lay in the ground beneath his feet, he would not live to make the enormous fortune he had dreamed of all his life.

*　*　*

Back in the village, we unpacked our kit and made ourselves comfortable in the hut, for from what Cetas had said, it seemed likely that we might have to stay several days before the crew of Brinsley's launch finished their carousing at Mount Everard and returned to take us up to Arakaka.

As we were doing so, Cetas arrived breathless in the hut. "Quick, quick," he cried, "dere's a big labaria down in de village. De men gwine to kill it, but I tell um you want to catch um."

Labaria is the local name for the fer-de-lance, one of the most dangerous and venomous of all the South American snakes. We ran out of the hut into the village, to find a circle of people standing at a very respectful distance from a two-foot-long snake of a nondescript sandy colour which lay somnolently at the foot of a palm tree. Jack pushed his way through the circle and looked hard at the snake.

"I don't think it is a labaria," he said. He picked up a long slender stick and took a step nearer. The snake did not move. Quite slowly Jack placed the stick flat across the snake's neck. The reptile suddenly came to life, but it was too late; its body writhed and thrashed, but it was unable to move its head. Jack, delicately but firmly, put a thumb and forefinger round its neck and picked it up.

"Eh! Take care, chief," cried Cetas, horror-struck. "Dat's a real bad snake you get. Dat's labaria."

"No, it's not labaria," said Jack, and gently opened its mouth with the point of a pencil. "In fact," he added, "it's not even poisonous. It's one of the fang-less family, though which one I don't really know."

He released his firm grip on the snake's neck and let it crawl freely over his arm.

"Ai! He bite you! You die! Dat's labaria!" yelled the watching villagers in terror.

"No, no. He get no teeth," Jack explained, gesturing in his mouth with his hand to make his meaning clear. The snake crawled up his arm, over his shoulder and round his neck. "He no labaria, he good snake."

"Chief, chief!" moaned Cetas softly. "He labaria; he waiting to bite you an' en you die."

"Now look, I show you that he good snake," said Jack patiently. He removed it from his neck and holding it by its tail dropped it head-first inside his shirt. "You see, he no bite at all."

The villagers were struck dumb. Cetas's jaw sagged open and a woman by him stuck her fist into her mouth and opened her eyes so wide that they seemed in danger of falling out. Jack, with the snake wriggling gently inside his shirt, walked back to the hut to find a box in which to keep it.

Unfortuately, two hours later he was called upon to display his knowledge of snakes in another way. As we sat eating in the hut, Brinsley McLeod appeared. He was supporting an Amerindian who limped pitifully, his face pallid and his eyes closed in pain.

"Dis man bitten by labaria on 'is ankle. I t'ink 'e die," Brinsley said.

"Get some cord and bandages, and a razor blade, quickly," said Jack. He helped the man to sit on the steps of the hut and looked at his ankle. "How long ago did this happen?" he asked Brinsley.

"'E say 'bout one hour. He walkin' 'long de path in de bush an' de labaria bite 'im. 'E say dat 'e kill de snake after it bite 'im an' den 'e come straight here."

Charles had produced what Jack required. Working swiftly, Jack applied a makeshift tourniquet just above the knee and then, taking the razor blade, he made four cross cuts deep into the flesh round the fang-mark. The blood spurted freely. Jack bent down and put his mouth to the wound. Three times he sucked and spat out a mouthful of blood. Then he dressed the wound, bandaged it and gave the man a sedative. Meanwhile, one of the villagers had slung a hammock in a hut next to ours. Jack carried the man over and laid him gently in it.

We walked back to Brinsley. "There was only one fang mark," Jack said, "and I may have sucked out a little of the poison, but I am afraid that an hour is a long time and there may be too much venom already circulating in his system for us to save him."

"I t'ought maybe you get dat special stuff fer snake bite, dat you put in wid a needle," said Brinsley.

"No," explained Jack, "that stuff no good except you get ice-box to keep it cold. As soon as it get warm, it worthless."

We kept a close watch on our patient. His pulse rate became weaker and weaker, but even more alarming, the blood dripped unceasingly from his sodden bandage, for one of the effects of the fer-de-lance venom is to prevent the coagulation of the blood, and no clot was therefore forming on the wound. Every twenty minutes, we had to remove the tourniquet so that the circulation in the leg was not permanently impaired, but we replaced it as soon as we dared, for without it the flow of blood from the wound increased alarmingly. It seemed that if the man did not die from the effects of the venom, he might die from loss of blood. The only hope was to get him down to the mouth of the Barima to Morawhanna. We could not do that until Brinsley's launch arrived.

All that day we watched over our patient as he lay groaning in his hammock, his bandaged foot oozing blood. We changed tourniquets and gave him hot sweetened coffee, but he refused all food and asked only for "cigreet".

The next morning his condition was unchanged. There was little we could do but wait for the launch to come. At five o'clock in the evening, to our relief it arrived. It was quite a large boat powered by a diesel engine, with four posts amidships supporting a small wooden roof. We tied a hammock diagonally from one post to another and carried the invalid down to the boat. We decided that all three of us should accompany him, for, transport being so unreliable on the river, we felt that if once we split up, we might have difficulty in uniting again. Brinsley himself agreed to pilot the launch and at half-past five, the four of us, with the Amerindian moaning in his hammock, set off for Morawhanna.

Travelling with the stream we made very good time and we reached Mount Everard in three hours. We stopped only for more fuel and then continued on our way.

It was now dark, but the moon had risen and in its light we could see that the character of the trees on the bank had changed; the tall forest trees had been replaced by mangroves, their gnarled roots arching out of the water in a black tangle.

The night was still warm, and as the swinging hammock occupied most of the space in the boat, Charles decided to climb on to the roof, spread a blanket and there go to sleep. We drove through the night.

Suddenly there was an appalling jolting crash. Branches thrashed along the side of the boat until it juddered to a standstill. We had run straight into the mangroves while going at full speed. My immediate thought was for Charles, and I leaped out upon the roof. Leaves and broken branches lay all over the roof and jagged stumps had scored great grooves in it. By some miracle, most of the bigger branches had missed Charles and he had received only one really heavy blow. It had caught him on the collar bone and although it had temporarily paralysed his arm there seemed to be no lasting damage. I helped him climb down in the dark.

Brinsley drove the boat astern. "I t'ink I fall asleep," he said apologetically.

An hour later, it became very cold and started to rain. We huddled miserably together, hugging our knees to our chests to keep warm, and trying to get a few minutes' sleep. But the deafening noise of the engine, the cold and the rain kept us all awake. At four o'clock in the morning we reached Morawhanna, roused a watchman on the jetty and found, to our astonishment, a telephone. Within twenty minutes an ambulance arrived, and fifteen minutes later our poor invalid was lying on a stretcher, being injected with anti-venine and penicillin by a white-coated doctor, while a nurse put a clean dressing on the foot.

We waited anxiously.

The doctor put down his hypodermic syringe and took the patient's pulse.

"I think he's going to be all right," he said. "There is nothing further we can do. Would you care to join me for breakfast?"

CHAPTER
ELEVEN

The Barima

Immediately after our breakfast with the doctor, we returned to the launch and began the long trip back to Koriabo. Brinsley told us that there were many people living along the banks of this part of the river and it occurred to Jack that if we stopped at each village to offer the inhabitants substantial rewards for animals, there was every hope that they might have captured something interesting by the time we came back down the river to catch the Georgetown boat six days hence.

We were all very tired, for none of us had slept for over twenty-four hours, so we took the job in turns. While two of us slept, one in the hammock and the other lying outstretched on the launch's roof, the third sat in the bows, ready to jump ashore at the next settlement and explain to the villagers what we wanted. Few of these places comprised more than two or three huts and often there was only one building surrounded by groves of coconut palms and fields of rice. The men that came out in reply to our hails were mostly East Indians. They looked at us uncomprehendingly as we explained with extravagant gestures what it was we wanted and how easy it would be to earn the dollars that we waved about.

Usually we climbed back on board certain in our own minds that the people ashore had not understood one word we had said.

It was not until late evening that we reached Koriabo. Cetas Kingston was there to meet us, together with the wife of the sick man. Suppressing any emotion she might feel, she asked us with an expressionless face if her husband was alive or dead. We told her that he was getting better and that he would soon be back in the village. She said nothing and walked back silently to her hut.

Next morning, Brinsley came to us with gloomy news. He could not take us up to Arakaka, he said, for the engine of his launch had broken down under the strain of running almost continuously for eighteen hours and it would have to be stripped and bathed in oil before it would work again. This description of the engine's ailment was not altogether convincing and we suspected that in reality it was Brinsley who was rather tired of steaming up and down the river. We could not blame him, and though our chances of getting to Arakaka now seemed extremely remote, we were not perturbed. Koriabo was a very pleasant village, the people were kind and helpful and we had seen many signs of abundant wild life in the surrounding forest.

The village, moreover, swarmed with tame animals. The prime pet-keeper was an old lady whom everyone affectionately called "Mama". Her hut was in itself a minor menagerie. Green Amazon parrots hopped along the roof, blue tanagers fluttered and sang in wicker-work cages swinging from the eaves, a pair of scruffy macaw chicks scuffled among the ashes of the fire and a capuchin monkey, tethered by a rope round his waist, haunted the gloomy interior.

We were sitting on the hut steps talking to Mama, when a most extraordinary high-pitched whistling giggle rose from the undergrowth just beyond. The grass parted and two enormous pig-like creatures gravely and ponderously stalked out. They came within a yard of us, sat down on their haunches and surveyed us with disdain. They looked at first sight like two large brown pigs, but their heads were very different for they possessed not a snout, but a nose so blunt that it was almost rectangular in profile. This gave them an extremely supercilious expression, the dignity of which was somewhat marred by their inappropriate giggles. They were capybara, the largest rodents in the world. I stretched out a hand to one of them and tried to stroke it, but it jerked up its head and snapped at my fingers.

"'E no 'urt," said Mama. "'E wanna suck."

Encouraged, I cautiously poked a finger at the creature's nose. It gave a whistling whinny, bared its bright orange incisor teeth and engulfed my finger in its mouth. As it sucked noisily, I felt my fingernail grating on what seemed to be two bony rasps half-way down its throat. Mama, whose pidgin English was limited, explained by elaborate dumb-show that she had caught the two creatures as tiny youngsters and had raised them on the bottle. They were now almost fully grown but they had never lost the habit of sucking anything that was offered to them. Each of them had a broad red stripe painted round its haunches and Mama told us that she had put it on, so that no hunter would shoot her pets as they rambled through the bush.

We asked if we might film them. Mama nodded and Charles set up the camera. Capybara are essentially amphibious animals and in the wild state they spend a great deal of their time in the river, emerging at night to graze on the vegetation of the banks. We were anxious, therefore, to photograph them swimming, and I tried to lure them down to the river. They whistled and giggled but stubbornly refused to go anywhere near the water. Enticement having failed, I tried to chase them into the river, remembering the natural history books which said "when alarmed capybara invariably take to water". Our two invariably took to a shady corner beneath Mama's hut. I became hotter and hotter as I ran up and down the village after the creatures, clapping my hands and shouting. Mama sat on the steps of her hut with a puzzled look on her face.

"It's no good," I panted to Charles, "the wretched things have obviously been tame so long that they have lost their taste for swimming."

A slow look of comprehension dawned on Mama's face.

"Swim?" she said.

"Yes, swim," I replied.

"Ah! swim," she said with a sunny smile. "Aieee!"

In answer to her piercing shriek, two naked little urchins got up from playing in the dust beneath the house and walked over to her.

"Swim!" she said.

The children skipped down to the river. The capybara

looked down their noses at us, turned and ambled after them. The children waited for the animals to arrive and then all four plunged in the water together and began to splash and wrestle, the children screaming with laughter.

Mama watched them with matronly complacency.

"I get all as babies together," she said, and went on to explain that from the beginning of their lives the four infants had always bathed together and that now the capybara would not go into the river without the children.

We had told Mama that, like her, we were fond of tame animals and that we were hoping to take many back to our own country. Mama looked at the capybara. "For me, dem too big," she said. "You wish take 'em? I able get more."

Jack was overjoyed at the offer, but a little uncertain as to how he would manage to transport such enormous creatures back to Georgetown. Eventually we arranged with Mama that we would try to get a cage built at Arakaka — if we ever got there — and collect the animals when we returned down the river.

Many of the other people in the village who possessed pets very understandably did not wish to part with them. One woman had a tame labba. It was a charming little creature with slender delicate legs like those of a miniature antelope. Like the capybara, it is a rodent and a relative of the guinea pig. Its coat was a rich brown, spotted with cream, and it gazed at us with lustrous black eyes as it lay in its owner's lap. The woman told us that three years earlier she had had a baby which had died in infancy. Soon afterwards her husband, hunting in the forest, had discovered a female labba with its young. He had shot the adult for food and brought the orphan back alive to his wife. She had taken the baby creature and suckled it at her own breast. Now it was fully grown. She stroked it affectionately. "'E my baby," she said simply.

Twenty yards away from the hut in which we were staying stood a large bush covered with purple-red flowers. Jack had noticed that it was visited every evening by many nectar-feeding birds and he decided to try and catch some of them with the aid of bird-lime. This substance had been brewed from forest plants, not in South America, but in Africa. Jack maintained that he had never found bird-lime so powerfully sticky as that which had been made for him by a native hunter whom he had met in West Africa. Accordingly, before every expedition he wrote to a friend in Sierra Leone who commissioned a hunter to prepare a large quantity of "sticky", as it is termed, and then sent it to Jack by post in a cocoa tin. This tin Jack carried with him wherever he went. Its contents were not a pleasant sight, for the bird-lime resembled rather dirty chewing gum, and to retain its power it had to be kept in a solution of lemon juice and water. Jack opened his tin, spat on his hands — "sticky" is conveniently powerless against anything coated in spittle — and drew it out in long thin ropes. These he wound round likely perching places on the bush. The process took upwards of an hour, and having completed it he retired to the hut to sit on the steps and watch the bush with his binoculars.

As the sun sank, the birds began to arrive to feed from the flowers of the bush. The most brilliant of them was a Blue Honey-creeper. About the size of a sparrow, it had a long curved bill, a cap of turquoise, a body of deep ultramarine, and jet black wings. It fluttered on to the tree and perched among a group of flowers that Jack had not been able to reach. We watched it anxiously through the binoculars. It fed for a few minutes, flew up to the top of the bush and looked around. Then it came down again and approached a part of the bush where Jack had put the "sticky". We held our breath. It cocked its head at a group of flowers and flew to them. As it came to settle on a twig, its feet touched the lime and it lost its balance, toppled over and hung motionless upside-down. Jack dashed down the steps, ran to the bush and gently put his hand round the elegant creature. With infinite care he delicately unstuck its legs and, spitting on his fingers, meticulously removed all traces of the lime from its little feet. He carried it tenderly back to the hut and released it in a large airy cage. It flew around for a few seconds and then settled on one of the perches. Within a few minutes it was finishing its evening meal from the bottle of honey solution hanging in the cage.

That evening, we were surprised to hear the throbbing of an engine. As dusk fell a large launch came round the bend of the river and moored by the village. The Indian captain in charge told us that he was bringing up stores and mail for the mining company and that the next day he would be continuing to Arakaka. He asked us if we would like to go with him, and we accepted readily: it seemed at last that we might reach our destination.

Early in the morning we carried our kit down to the launch. We explained to Mama that we would be back in four days' time to collect the capybara, and Brinsley promised to repair his boat so that he could take us down to Morawhanna when we returned. Most of the mining company's launch was occupied by freight, and there was one other passenger, a fat jolly negress who was introduced to us as Gertie. Nevertheless there was plenty of room for us, and after the tiny dug-out canoe and Brinsley's small boat, we thought it luxurious. We lay back in the bows and all three of us drifted off to sleep.

At four o'clock that afternoon we arrived at Arakaka. From the river it looked a charming and idyllic place; a string of small houses perched on the high bank, backed by tall sheafs of feathery bamboo swaying in the wind. When we landed, however, the charm dissolved. Two-thirds of the houses were stores combined with rum-parlours and behind them, in muddy squalor, stood the dilapidated wooden shanties in which the villagers lived.

Fifty years ago, Arakaka had been a flourishing community of several hundred people. There had been rich gold mines in the bush nearby and it was said that the mining managers of those days used to drive with their wives in coaches along the main street. Now the gold mines were worked out and the street was grass. Most of the houses had fallen down, rotted and been reclaimed by the forest. An air of dissolution and degeneracy hung over the atrophied town as it mouldered in the heat. Near one of the shanties we found, submerged beneath a blanket of creepers, a weathered wooden table. Its feet were still embedded in decaying mortar and it stood on a platform of brickwork which was cracked and riven by the roots of the plants which concealed it. "De hospital stood here," we were told, "and dat's de old mortuary table."

Although it was the middle of the afternoon the rum shops were already full and an old gramophone was blaring out tinny music. We went into one of the shops. A tall muscular young negro sat on a bench with an enamel mug full of rum in his hand.

"Wha' you come up dis way for, man?" he asked.

We said we were looking for animals.

"Well dere's plenty here," he said, "an' Ah kin catch 'em easy."

"Splendid," Jack replied. "We will pay well for anything you bring us, but we are only here for a few days, so will you catch us something to-morrow?"

The man wagged a finger solemnly in Jack's face.

"Ah cain't get anyt'ing to-morrow," he said gravely, "'cause to-morrow Ah'se goin' to be drunk."

Gertie, our fellow passenger on the launch, strolled into the shop.

She leaned on the counter and looked hard in the Chinese storekeeper's eyes.

"Mistah," she said soulfully, "de boys on de launch is telling me dat dere's plenty vampire bats up here. What kin I do, 'cause I ain't got no moskeeta net fo' my hammock?"

"You ain't bothered 'bout vampires, is you, ma?" said the negro with the enamel mug.

"Ah certainly is," she replied stoutly. "Ma psychological disposition is highly nervous."

The negro blinked hard. Gertie switched her attentions back to the storekeeper.

"Now what you got to give me?" she said, with a simpering smile.

"I ain't got nothing to give, ma; but for two dollar I can sell you a lamp. That will keep the vampires away for sure."

"Really mistah," she said with exaggerated hauteur, "I mus' add dat my financial basis is of de mos' very meagre." She gave a gurgling laugh. "Gimme a two-cent candle."

Later that evening, my psychological disposition, like Gertie's, also became highly nervous and for the same reason. We were staying in a decaying rest-house near the store. Jack and Charles went to sleep quickly underneath their mosquito nets, but I unfortunately had mislaid mine and for the past four days had been without one. Accordingly, because of Gertie's warning of vampires, I hung a lighted paraffin lamp at the end of my hammock. Ten minutes later, as I lay trying to sleep, a bat silently flapped in through the open window. It flew over my hammock, round the room, into the passage, back again under my hammock and out of the window. Every two minutes it came in and repeated this flight with unnerving regularity.

Without catching it, I could not be certain that it was a vampire, but in such circumstances, zoological niceties are not necessary for conviction.

It did not seem to possess the elaborate leaf-shaped

structure on its nose which many harmless bats have and which vampires lack, and although I could not see them, I felt sure it was armed with the pair of triangular razor-sharp front teeth with which vampires shave a thin section of skin from their victim. Having made the wound, they will squat by it and lap up the exuding blood. This they are able to do without disturbing a man's sleep, so that in the morning the only sign of their visitation is a blood-soaked blanket, though three weeks later the man may develop the dreadful disease of paralytic rabies.

I found it difficult to believe implicitly in the storekeeper's assurance that vampires will never settle to feed where there is light, and my fears seemed to be justified when it suddenly settled in the far corner of the room and, in typical vampire fashion, began to scuttle around on the floor, its wings folded back along its forearms, so that it resembled some foul four-legged spider. I could stand it no longer. I reached below my hammock, picked up one of my boots and hurled it at the beast. It took to flight and disappeared through the window.

Within twenty minutes I was feeling almost grateful to the vampire, for the thought of it kept me awake for a long time and as a result I was able to achieve something which had become an obsession with me over the past few weeks: the recording of one of the most eerie sounds of the South American forest.

I had first heard this noise on our trip up the Kukui. We had pitched camp in the forest by the river and slung our hammocks between the trees. As we went to sleep the light of the stars twinkled through the leaves above. The ghostly shapes of bushes and creepers loomed around us. Suddenly, throbbing and echoing through the forest came an ululating yell rising in great crescendoes of blood-chilling loudness and then dying away to a moan like the sound of a gale wailing through telegraph wires. This terrifying noise was produced by nothing more fearsome than the howler monkey. The real function of these nocturnal choruses is not really known, but it is certain that the howler monkey is able to produce one of the loudest noises of any animal on earth.

For weeks I had tried to record it. Every night that we were in the forest I had religiously fitted a microphone into a parabolic sound reflector, and loaded the recorder with new tape. Night after night we would hear nothing. Then one evening we would get to camp very late and very tired, and I would be too exhausted to set up the apparatus. That night, inevitably, I would be woken by the monkeys in full cry; I would jump from my hammock and frantically begin assembling the apparatus. As soon as everything was ready to be switched on, the chorus would stop. Once, on the Kukui, I thought that I had achieved success. The monkeys were so close that the noise was deafening and for once the recording apparatus was ready. I switched it on and for several minutes recorded the most brilliant and terrifying howls I had heard. When the performance finished with two final yapping barks, I triumphantly wound back the tape and roused Charles from his hammock to hear it. The entire tape was blank; one of the valves had broken during the day's journey.

Now, at last, thanks to the vampire bat, I was awake right at the beginning of a chorus. The monkeys were probably half a mile away but even so the noise was extremely loud. I lugged the equipment out of the rest-house, set everything up and carefully aimed my parabolic reflector in the direction from which the sound was coming. After my previous experience I did not play the tape back to Charles until the morning. We listened to it together. The recording was perfect.

That morning the mining manager drove into Arakaka from his camp twelve miles away in the forest. He had received our message by radio but he was nonetheless a little surprised to see us, and explained that he could not take us out to his camp that day as his small truck would be piled high with the goods which had been brought up on the launch. However, he suggested that we might lunch with him the next day and promised to send a truck in to collect us.

We spent the rest of the day rambling in the forest near the town. Jack was hoping to find some interesting millipedes and scorpions, and, coming across a low palm-like tree, he began tearing off the dry brown leaf-husks that wrapped round its trunk. As he did so there was a loud hissing noise and a golden brown furry creature, the size of a small dog, uncurled from the upper part of the tree and hastily scrambled down the opposite side of the trunk. It was on the ground and lumbering away before we could get near it. It could not run fast, however, and with a few strides Jack overtook it and picked it up by its stout, almost naked tail. It hung upside down, glared furiously at us with its little beady eyes, and hissed and dribbled through its long curved snout. Jack was jubilant, for by sheer good fortune he had found a tamandua, the tree anteater.

We carried it back to the rest-house in triumph and while Jack began preparing a cage for it, we parked it in a tall tree close to the rest-house. The tamandua clasped the trunk with its forelegs and clambered up with rapidity and ease. When it was some twenty feet from the ground it stopped, turned round and gave us an angry look. Then it noticed that a few feet away hung a large globular ants' nest. Forgetting its irritation, it clambered towards the nest and, wrapping its prehensile tail round a branch just above, hung head downwards. With swift powerful swipes of its forelegs it ripped open the nest. A brown flood of ants flowed out of the gash and swarmed all over the tamandua, which, not in the least dismayed, stuck its tube-like snout into the hole and began licking up the ants with its long black tongue. After five minutes it absent-mindedly began to scratch itself with its hind leg as it feasted. Soon it was scratching with one of its forelegs as well. Finally it decided that further food was not worth the penalty of additional ant stings, and it made a leisurely retreat. Its thick wiry fur was obviously not the complete protection against ants that it is often supposed to be, for at every other step the tamandua had to stop and scratch.

Charles and I sat watching and filming its progress when it occurred to us that the task of climbing the tree to recapture the tamandua was not going to be a pleasant one. Angry ants were swarming all over the branches, and if the tamandua found their bites irritating, we should no doubt find them extremely painful. Fortunately the anteater solved the problem for us, for it scrambled down the tree and sat on the ground, rubbing its right ear with its back leg. The biting ants kept it so busy that it allowed Jack to pick it up and put it in the cage. There it squatted peaceably in a corner and set about removing ants from its left ear.

That night we went hunting with torches. In the darkness the forest seemed an eerie, mysterious place full of unseen yet noisy activity. The texture of the sound varied from place to place; by the river, frogs filled the air with a metallic clinking, but as we moved further into the forest, the whirrs and chirps of insects became predominant. We quickly became accustomed to this unceasing chorus but the sudden crash of a falling tree or an echoing unidentifiable shriek brought my heart into my mouth.

Paradoxically, we were able to find things in the darkness which we would never have seen in daylight, for all animals' eyes act as reflectors, and as the beam of our torches fell on a creature looking in our direction, we saw two little lights shining back at us through the darkness. The size, colour and spacing of these eyes enabled us to make a guess at what animal we had found.

As we shone our torches over the surface of the river, we counted four pairs of glowing red coals — caiman lying almost submerged with their eyes just above the surface of the water. High in a tree we detected a monkey which, wakened by our steps, had turned to look at us. The reflections from its eyes disappeared momentarily as it blinked; then they vanished altogether and we heard a crash — it had turned its back on us and fled away through the branches.

Treading as silently as we could, we approached a thicket of bamboo, the stems creaking and groaning as they swayed in the darkness thirty feet above us. Jack shone his torch into the spiny tangle at the base of the clump.

"A good place for snakes," he said with enthusiasm. "You go round to the other side and see if you can scare anything out towards me."

I picked my way with caution through the darkness and began beating against the bamboo with my machete. As I did so, the light from my torch fell upon a small hole in the ground.

"Jack," I called softly. "There's a small hole here."

"I dare say there is," he answered a trifle testily, "but is there anything in it?"

Gingerly I knelt down and looked. From the depths of the hole three bright little eyes glowed at me.

"There most certainly is," I called back. "And what is more, it has got three eyes!"

Jack was by my side within a few seconds and together we peered down the hole. With the light of our two torches, we saw, crouching at the bottom, a black hairy spider as big as my hand. The eyes I had seen were only three of the eight that sparkled on the top of its ugly head. Menacingly, it raised its two front legs, exposing the iridescent blue pads with which they were tipped and giving us a clear view of its large curved poison fangs.

"A beauty," Jack murmured. "Don't let him jump out," and he put his torch on the ground while he fumbled in his pocket for a cocoa tin. I picked up a twig and gently pushed it down the side of the hole. The spider lashed out with its front legs and pounced on it.

"Careful," said Jack. "If you rub any of that hair from its body, it won't live for very long."

He gave me the tin. "You hold that at the mouth of the hole and I'll see if I can persuade it to walk out." Reaching over, he carefully pressed his knife into the ground so that the earth shook at the back of the hole. The spider revolved to face the new danger and retreated a few steps. Jack twisted the knife in the ground. The back of the hole crumbled and the spider suddenly ran backwards and landed straight in the tin. Quickly, I slipped on the lid.

Jack grinned with satisfaction and put the tin safely back into his pocket.

The next day would have to be our last at Arakaka, for our boat was due to leave Morawhanna at the mouth of the Barima in three days' time, and it would take us two days to get there. The mining company's jeep was due to come at mid-day to collect us and take us out to the camp twelve miles away. As we waited for it, we speculated with enthusiasm about the animals we should find when we arrived. But the jeep did not come on time and it was late afternoon before the manager drove in, full of apologies, to explain that the truck had broken down and had only just been repaired: it was now too late for us to visit the camp. We asked what animals might have been ours, had we been able to get there.

"Well," he said, "we did have a sloth but it died, and there was a monkey but that has now escaped. Still, I'm sure we could find a few parrots knocking about."

We heard this with mixed feelings, disappointed at having come so far in pursuit of so little, but relieved that we had not missed anything spectacular by failing, at the last moment, to reach the camp.

The manager climbed back into his jeep and drove out of Arakaka. We were now faced with the problem of finding a boat to take us back down the river. We visited all the rum-parlours in turn. There were many people who had canoes with outboard engines but everyone had a very good reason for not carrying us: the engine was broken, the canoe too small, there was no fuel, or the only man who really *understood* the engine was not in Arakaka at the moment. At last we discovered, sitting morosely in one of the rum-parlours, an East Indian named Jacob. It would have been difficult not to notice him, for the tops of his ears sprouted long tufts of straight black hair which gave him the look of a dismal oriental leprechaun. Jacob admitted that he had a boat, but said he could not take us. However, unlike everyone else he did not seem to be able to think of any good reason to support his decision and we pressed our case. We argued and haggled in the tobacco-laden atmosphere of the rum-parlour while a gramophone screeched in our ears. At about half-past ten, Jacob's resistance finally broke down, and with infinite gloom he agreed to take us to Koriabo in the morning.

We rose at six and were packed and ready to leave at seven. Jacob was nowhere to be seen. At nine o'clock he walked miserably up to the rest-house and announced that he had the boat and the engine was all ready, but that he had not yet been able to find any petrol.

Gertie, having nothing else to do, was standing nearby, following the conversation with interest. She looked at me sympathetically and heaved a heavy sigh.

"Maan," she said, "ain't it turrible all dis procrastination. It's real vexatious."

By mid-day, however, the engine was fuelled and at last we set off down river for Koriabo. The tamandua lay curled asleep in its cage with half an ants' nest lying by it for refreshment on the journey. Straddling the bows and overlapping an ample two feet on either side perched a large wooden cage which Jack had had made at Arakaka ready for the capybaras.

It was extremely fortunate that we were travelling with the swift current of the swollen river, for Jacob's outboard engine was capricious to a degree and would brook no interference of any sort. If a small piece of floating wood temporarily blocked the inlet of the water-cooling system, or if we required it to run at anything but full throttle, then it stopped, and having stopped needed considerable coaxing to persuade it to start again. Jacob had only one method of doing this, and that was to pull the starting rope with maximum force as frequently as possible; the internal works of his engine were sacrosanct and must on no account be interfered with. His faith was always eventually justified, though on one occasion he had to pull the starting rope non-stop for an hour and a half. When it finally restarted Jacob, who had been gritting his teeth in subdued fury, betrayed no sign of triumph, but sat down at the tiller and relapsed into his normal state of deep gloom.

We reached Koriabo in the late afternoon and moored alongside Brinsley McLeod's launch. Jacob did not wish to stop the engine unnecessarily, so we unloaded as quickly as possible. Within ten minutes the canoe was empty, and Jacob, uncheered by the considerable achievement of completing the operation without stalling the engine, had dismally started on his way back to Arakaka.

We learned to our relief that Brinsley's launch was once more in running order, and although he himself was out of the village working his gold claim in the back-dam, we were assured that he would come back to the village at ten o'clock the next morning.

Somewhat to our surprise, he did. We enticed the capybaras into their cage by filling it with over-ripe pineapples and cassava bread, and loaded it on board for our final day's travel down the Barima. The journey was a long one, for we stopped at all the little settlements we had visited on our way up to see if anyone had caught any animals, as we had asked. Several people had done so, and by the time we reached Mount Everard we had on board with us, in addition to the tamandua, the capybaras and the snake, three macaws, five parrots, two parakeets, a capuchin monkey and, best of all, a pair of red billed toucans. The bargaining inherent in the acquisition of all these creatures delayed us so much that darkness fell while we were still ten miles from Morawhanna and it was one o'clock in the morning when we finally nosed in alongside s.s. *Tarpon*, lying by the jetty at Morawhanna.

We clambered up the gangway and went on board. After picking our way among the sleeping bodies that littered the decks, we eventually discovered the chief steward's cabin. He emerged, clad only in a pair of vividly-striped pyjamas, but when he discovered that he had official functions to discharge, he jammed his peaked cap on his head and showed us to two cabins which, miraculously, had been reserved for us. We filled one with animals, and, at half-past two, the three of us wearily climbed into the bunks of the other.

When I next opened my eyes, it was mid-day; we were at sea and Georgetown lay on the horizon ahead.

CHAPTER TWELVE

Hoatzins and Mermaids

Several surprises awaited us in the garage which held Tim Vinall's menagerie in Georgetown, for while we had been away on the Barima, our friends in other parts of the Colony had sent us more animals. The amphibian plane had recently visited Kamarang, and the pilot had brought back for us several parakeets and a tame red-capped woodpecker as a gift from Bill and Daphne Seggar. Tiny McTurk had sent a savannah fox and a bag containing several snakes. Tim, not content with the full-time job of looking after the collection, had also encouraged local people to bring in what animals they could find. Several had come from the Botanic Garden itself. A gardener had caught a pair of mongoose, families of which we had seen scampering over the lawns. Tim was glad to have them, although they are not strictly South American animals. They were imported many years ago from India by sugar planters in the hope that they would keep down the plagues of rats which caused so much damage among the sugar cane; since then they have increased in numbers so greatly that they now are one of the commonest animals along the coast. The gardens were also swarming with opossums, creatures which, like kangaroos, carry their newly-born young in a pouch. I had been very eager to see this animal, one of the very few marsupials that are found outside Australasia, but I was sadly disappointed. Tim's two looked like enormous rats with pointed snouts almost naked of fur, long sharp teeth and repulsive scaly tails. They were without doubt the most hideous animals in the entire collection. Tim told us with glee that he had unhesitatingly christened them David and Charles.

Most remarkable of all these additions was a bad-tempered snivelling beast called Percy. Percy was a tree porcupine and like all members of the porcupine family, he was exceedingly ill-tempered. If anyone tried to touch him he screwed up his little face, rattled his short quills and hissed and stamped with rage, leaving it in no doubt that he would be delighted to use his long front teeth on anyone who came too near. His bristly tail was prehensile and with it he could grip onto branches as he climbed. Many tree-living animals are similarly equipped, but most of them — monkeys, pangolins, opossums and tamandua anteaters — possess tails which roll downwards. Percy's rolled upwards, a distinction he shared with, of all things, some mice living in Papua.

In spite of the addition of all these new creatures and the ones we had brought from the Barima, there still remained two important gaps in the collection, two extremely interesting Guyanese creatures which we had not yet caught. The first was a bird, the hoatzin. To scientists it is of particular interest for, unique among birds, it possesses claws on its wings. In the adult, these are useless and buried deep in the wing feathers, but they are fully functional in the unfledged chick which uses its clawed wings as a second pair of legs to enable it to clamber in the branches round its nest. Fossils indicate that birds developed from reptilian ancestors, and ornithologists used to believe that the hoatzin was a primitive bird which still retained the claws of its forebears — that it represented a link between reptiles and birds. More recent researches, however, have gone to show that the claws of the hoatzin are not relics, but relatively modern developments. Either way, the bird is unique, and the only place in the world where it is to be found is on the coasts of this part of South America.

The second animal we wanted so badly was a large seal-like mammal called the manatee which spends its life in the creeks inoffensively browsing on weeds. Being a mammal, it suckles its young and does so by rearing out of the water, holding its single offspring to its breast, cradled in its flippers. It has been said that descriptions of the creature doing this, brought back by the first seamen to sail round the coasts of South America, gave rise to the legend of the mermaid.

We were told that both the hoatzin and the manatee were quite common in the Canje River a few miles down the coast from Georgetown. We had one week left in which to catch them, and so two days after we had returned from the Barima, we set off once more, this time by train, to the little town of New Amsterdam which lies at the mouth of the Canje.

British Guyana became British only at the beginning of the nineteenth century. For several hundred years previously it had been governed by Holland, and as our train rattled along the coast signs of the Dutch occupation were still plain to see. The railway stations were named after the huge sugar estates they serviced — Beterverwagting, Weldaad, and Onverwagt. Many of the estates themselves owe their existence to the sea wall, far away on our left, which the Dutch built to convert the barren salt marshes into rich productive land, and in New Amsterdam itself, sweltering on the edge of the mile-wide estuary of the Berbice River, we saw, mingled with modern concrete buildings and wooden bungalows, a few elegant, white-painted houses — evidence of the dignity of the Dutch colonial architecture.

It seemed to us that the most likely people to help us in our search would be fishermen, so we went down to the harbour. Africans and East Indians sat mending nets and gossiping in their small wooden boats moored by the jetty. We asked if anyone could help us to catch a "water-mamma" as the manatee is called locally. No one volunteered to do so, but everyone seemed to think that the man to help us was an African named "Mistah King".

He, it appeared, was a man of many parts. By profession he was a fisherman, but his strength was so prodigious that he was much in demand throughout New Amsterdam for all sorts of jobs such as pile-driving, which no other man could do properly. His recreation, we were told, was to "wrassle" with cows. He was also a great hunter and knew more about the wild life of the district than anyone else. If there was one man who could catch a manatee, it was Mr. King. We set off to look for him.

We found him at last sitting in the fish market, arguing with a trader about his catch. His appearance was startling enough to support his reputation. Immensely stout, he wore a brilliant red shirt, black pin-stripe trousers, and on top of his mop of frizzy hair a very small black homburg hat. We asked him if he could catch a manatee for us. "Well, man," he said, fondling his luxuriant side-whiskers, "dere is plenty in dese parts, but is very difficult to catch 'cause de water-mamma is de mos' pash'nate creature. When she get in de net, she fly into de mos' tur'ble passion an' t'row herself about an' she so strong dat she will bust open de strongest net."

"What do you do about that?" Jack asked.

"Dere is only one t'ing to do," said Mr. King sombrely. "When de water-mamma fust get in de net, you mus' stroke de net ropes so dat vibrations go down t'ru de water to de water-mamma. If you do dat right, she like it so much dat she jus' lie dere widout moving an' go oooh!" Mr. King emitted an expressive and ecstatic noise with a seraphic smile on his face. "I only know one man who can do dat," he added, "an' dat is me."

We were so impressed by this display of expertise that we engaged Mr. King on the spot. We had already arranged to hire a launch the next day, and Mr. King agreed to bring two assistants and his net first thing in the morning to begin the hunt.

The launch was manned by an African captain and an East Indian engineer, and we soon discovered that neither of them held Mr. King in as much awe as we had expected. After half an hour's travel up the Canje River, we saw an iguana high in one of the trees.

"Dere you are, Mr. King," said Rangur, the engineer. "How'se 'bout catchin' dat?"

Mr. King, with a lordly gesture, indicated that the launch should stop while he did so. He heaved his great weight into the dinghy, and with one of his assistants pushed off through the reeds to the base of the tree. The iguana, a splendid lizard about four feet long, lay immobile along a surprisingly thin branch, his green scales glinting in the sunlight fifteen feet above. Mr. King cut a tall bamboo and attached a noose to the end. This he hoisted and waved in front of the iguana's head.

"Wha' for you do dat, Mr. King?" called Fraser, the captain, with mock solemnity. "You t'ink maybe he's gwine to climb down it into your han's?"

The reptile sat motionless, oblivious of what was happening beneath.

"Hey, Mr. King," taunted Rangur, "dat be tame iguana dat you tied to de tree last night to give yourself a good name."

Mr. King, however, was above answering such ignorant jibes and instructed his assistant to climb the tree and guide the noose round the iguana's neck. The reptile responded to this by clambering lazily onto a higher branch.

"I t'ink," said Fraser, "dat de varmint is gwine to get de inclination to jump."

Mr. King exhorted his assistant to climb higher. For ten minutes the iguana, swaying in the breeze, permitted the noose to be dangled in front of it. Once it good-naturedly licked the rope as it swung close to its nose, but in spite of Mr. King's encouraging shouts it refused to stick its head in the noose. Finally, the man in the tree got too close. The iguana's patience was exhausted, and with exaggerated unconcern it turned aside from the rope and dived gracefully through the air into the river. The last we saw of it was a muddy swirl in the depths of the reed thicket.

"I t'ink," said Fraser to the world in general, "dat he got de inclination."

Mr. King returned to the boat.

"Dere's plenty more dem t'ings," he said. "We able to get plenty."

The banks of the river were lined with high barricades of the giant mucka-mucka reed. Its stems, as thick as my arm and so spongily cellular that I could sever them with an idle swipe of my machete, rose straight and naked, until fifteen feet above the water, they sprouted a few arrow-shaped leaves, and here and there a green fruit the size and shape of a pineapple. The leaves of the mucka-mucka we knew to be the favourite food of the hoatzins and we searched anxiously with the binoculars as we passed.

It was now mid-day. The sun beat down on us savagely. The metal fittings on the launch deck became too hot to touch. There was no breath of wind, and the leaves of the mucka-mucka hung motionless in the stifling heat, which shimmered over the river. Nothing stirred.

We saw our first hoatzin at about one o'clock. Jack's attention had been attracted by a muffled squawk rising from the mucka-mucka. Fraser stopped the launch, and through Jack's binoculars we were just able to distinguish the outline of a large bird sitting panting in the shade of the reeds. As we drifted closer, we saw another and then a third. Soon we realized that the whole thicket was full of birds taking refuge from the broiling sun.

It was four o'clock before we had a clear view of a hoatzin. The sun had sunk considerably and the heat was less oppressive. We rounded a bend in the river and saw a party of six birds feeding on the mucka-mucka leaves. They were handsome, chestnut-brown creatures, the size of chickens, with heavy bodies and thin necks. Their heads were crowned with a tall spiky crest of feathers, and their glittering red eyes were surrounded by naked blue skin. As we approached, they ceased feeding and watched us, nervously jerking their tails up and down and uttering harsh grating cries. At last they flapped heavily a few feet farther into the thicket and subsided into its depth; but not before Charles had filmed them.

We were thrilled to have seen these rare and beautiful birds, but our main interest was to watch the unique climbing behaviour of the chicks, so as we chugged slowly up the river, Jack continued to scour the reeds with his binoculars in search of a nest. We found one in the late afternoon. It was a flimsy platform of twigs hanging seven feet above the water in a thorn bush which grew among the mucka-mucka. Excitedly we clambered into the dinghy and paddled towards the bush. Two naked little chicks squatting on the nest peered over the edge, watching us. As we got closer their curiosity changed to fear and the scrawny wizened little creatures left the nest and groggily clambered up through the thorns, frantically gripping with their legs and their clawed wings. It was an astonishing and quite un-bird-like performance. As they clung to thin branches swaying above us, I stood up and gently reached towards them. Having demonstrated so perfectly their climbing ability, they then performed a trick which they alone among chicks can execute. They suddenly launched themselves into the air and dived neatly into the water nine feet below. They entered the water with hardly a splash, and as we watched, they swam energetically beneath the surface and disappeared deep into the thorny tangle.

We were disappointed that they had gone so soon for we had had no chance to photograph them, but we felt confident that as we had found chicks so easily on our first day there must be many more elsewhere on the river. Our search went on intensively for the rest of the time we spent on the Canje. We found several nests which contained eggs and one in particular was ideally suited to photography. As we approached it, the parent fluttered off heavily but soon returned, edging her way down the thin branch with her toes turned inwards like a tight-rope walker. As she sat, she did not settle herself with a wriggle on to her eggs, but squatted uncomfortably on them in a seemingly haphazard way.

We returned to visit her many times over the next few days in the hope that her eggs might have hatched, but they had still not done so when the time came for us to return to Georgetown and we never saw any chicks other than those that had entranced us on our first day.

Early on the evening of our first day we reached a point on the river where it was joined by a small creek. This was the perfect place for catching manatee, Mr. King told us. In half an hour the tide would turn and water would flow strongly down the creek into the Canje, carrying with it the lazy manatee which habitually grazed on its luxuriant weeds. All that had to be done to catch them was to stretch a net across the mouth of the creek. Accordingly, he plunged posts into the mud of the river bed on either side of the creek and stretched his net from one to the other. Then he sat in the dinghy alongside with his black homburg still in place, puffing at his pipe and awaiting the opportunity to display his remarkable rope-stroking skill.

After two hours he gave up. "No good," he said, "de tide not strong enough and no water come down. I know better place where we catch 'em to-night."

So the nets were hauled on board, the dinghy tied to the launch's stern and we moved on up the river. At dusk we reached the jetty of a sugar plantation. The over-ripe sickly-sweet smell of molasses drifted over the river as we moored. Rangur appeared from the galley with a steaming dish of rice and shrimps. After the meal Mr. King explained with a martyred air that we could now go to sleep; he would catch the manatee during the night and show it to us in the morning. We, however, wanted to see how it was done, so we asked if he would rouse us before he began.

"Maan," he said, "you don' wanna come wid me. I'se gwine to be working at two — three o'clock."

We assured him that we did but it was only with the greatest reluctance that he finally agreed to wake us.

The insects on the river swarmed thicker than we had

ever seen them. There were sand-flies, kaboura flies, mosquitoes, and, a novel addition, large hornets. They swarmed in through the hatches and circled our lamp in a dense cloud. Others, not having found the entrance, collected on the outside of the portholes in such numbers that they completely covered the glass in an opaque scum. Charles, being in charge of our medicine chest, looked out a large pot of insect-repellent ointment ready for the night's operations. We hung our mosquito nets, climbed into our bunks and went to sleep.

It was Jack who roused us at two o'clock for the manatee hunt. We dressed carefully in long-sleeved shirts, tucked our trousers into our stockings and as an additional protection against the insects liberally daubed our hands and faces with ointment. We clambered aft to see if Mr. King was ready. We found him lying on his back in his hammock, his mouth wide open, snoring stridently.

Jack shook him gently. Mr. King opened his eyes.

"Wha' for you do dat, man?" he said aggrievedly. "Is de middle of de night. I'se asleep."

"What about catching the water-mamma?"

"Cain't you see? Is too dark. Dere's no moon an' I cain't catch water-mamma in de dark, can I?" And with that he shut his eyes.

As we were up and dressed we decided that whether Mr. King came or not we might as well do a little hunting on our own account. There were obviously plenty of caiman in the river for, flashing our torches over the inky surface of the water, we saw several pairs of tell-tale lights glowing back at us. We climbed into the dinghy, cast off and drifted silently down the river. Charles and I sat in the stern paddling as noiselessly as we could, while Jack squatted in the bows, torch in hand. Slowly we glided towards the reeds fringing the bank. There was nothing to be heard but the distant croaking of frogs and the occasional high-pitched whine of mosquitoes. Jack slowly moved his torch beam over the surface of the water. Then, abruptly, he ceased waving it and shone it steadily on a patch of reeds. He signalled to us to stop paddling.

Quietly we shipped our paddles and the boat drifted imperceptibly closer and closer to the reed bed. Soon we could distinguish in the torch-light the glistening scaly head of a caiman lying just above the surface of the water facing us. Holding his torch steadily in the beast's eyes, Jack slowly leaned over the bows. As he did so his foot touched a baling tin in the bottom of the boat. There was a faint clatter and a swirl in the water ahead of us. Jack sat back and turned to us.

"I t'ink," he said, "dat de varmint got de inclination."

We began paddling again and within five minutes Jack had spotted another. Once again we glided towards it but when we were about ten yards away Jack switched off the beam of his torch.

"We'll forget about that one," he said. "Judging from the space between his eyes he is about seven feet long, and I'm not going to try and catch him barehanded."

Soon, however, we had discovered a third. Once again we repeated the approach, sliding silently over the glassy black surface of the river, our attention riveted to the pool of light cast by Jack's torch and the two red unwinking lights in its centre.

"Come and hold my feet," Jack whispered.

Charles moved quietly down the boat and clasped his ankles. As the boat drifted slowly towards the bedazzled caiman, Jack once again hung over the side. We got closer and closer until, from where I sat in the stern, the eyes of the caiman disappeared from my sight beneath the bows. Suddenly there was a splash, and a triumphant "Got him" from Jack. He dropped his torch into the boat and hung over the gunwale, grappling with the caiman with both hands.

"Hang on for heaven's sake," he called frantically to Charles, who was by now sitting on Jack's ankles and craning over the side himself. After tremendous splashings and gruntings Jack eventually leaned back into the boat, grinning. In his hands he grasped a snapping, struggling caiman over four feet long. While he held it by the scruff of the neck with his right hand, he tucked the creature's long scaly tail underneath his arm. The caiman hissed ferociously and opened its formidable jaws, exposing the leathery yellow inside of its mouth.

"I brought your kit bag along as I thought it might be useful," Jack explained hastily to me. "Would you mind passing it?" There seemed no time to argue, so I handed it to him. While I held it open, Jack carefully put the caiman inside and pulled the ropes of the bag tight.

"Well, that's something to show Mr. King, anyway," he said.

*   *   *

We spent three more days cruising on the Canje River with Mr. King and his crew, searching for manatee. We set nets at night, we set them during the day; we set them in the rain and in sunshine, when the tide ebbed and when the tide flowed, but never did we see any sign whatsoever of our quarry in spite of assurances that each of these conditions in turn was essential for our purpose. Finally we had no more provisions to stay out longer, so dolefully we sailed back to New Amsterdam.

"Well, man," said Mr. King philosophically as we paid him off, "I reckon we get bad luck."

As we walked away along the jetty, an East Indian fisherman ran up to us.

"You de men dat want water-mamma," he said, "'cause I get one t'ree days ago."

"What did you do with her?" we asked excitedly.

"I put she in a small lake just outside the town. I easily catch, if you want."

"Fine," said Jack, "we most certainly do. Let's go and catch her now."

The East Indian ran back along the jetty, loaded his net onto a hand-truck and collected three friends to assist him.

As our little procession wended its way through the crowded streets, I heard the word "water-mamma" being passed excitedly from person to person and by the time we reached the outskirts of the town and approached the meadow in which the lake lay, we had a large shouting crowd trailing behind us.

The lake was wide and muddy, but fortunately it was not deep. Everyone squatted on the banks and silently stared at the water, searching for a sign of the mermaid's position. Suddenly someone pointed to a mysteriously moving lotus leaf. It crumpled and vanished beneath the surface, and a few seconds later a brown muzzle appeared above the water, emitted a blast of air from two large circular nostrils and disappeared.

"'E dere. 'E dere," everyone shouted.

Narian, the fisherman, marshalled his forces. With his three assistants, he jumped into the water. Holding the long net stretched between them, he arranged them in a long line across the small bay where the manatee had been seen. Slowly, chest deep in the water, they advanced towards the bank. As they approached, the manatee betrayed her position by once more coming up for air. Narian yelled to the men on the two ends of the net to wade quickly to the bank and climb out so that the net formed not a straight line, but an arc. Now thoroughly disturbed, the manatee rose closer to the surface and rolled over, giving us a view of her great dun-brown flank.

A gasp of astonishment and pleasure rose from the crowd. "She big t'ing! Maan, she *monstrous*!"

Excitement gripped Narian's assistants on the bank and, enthusiastically aided by some of the onlookers, they began feverishly to haul in the net hand over hand. Narian, still wading in the lake, shouted furiously above the hubbub.

"Stop pullin'," he yelled. "No so fast."

No one took the slightest notice.

"Hundred dollar, de net," Narian screamed. "'E go bust if you no stop pulling."

But the crowd, having seen the manatee's flank once again, were obsessed by the desire to land her as quickly as possible, and they continued to haul in the net until the manatee lay enmeshed in the water just below the bank. She was obviously a very big one, but there was no time to see more for she suddenly arched her body and thrashed with her enormous tail, soaking everyone in muddy water. The net broke and she disappeared. Narian's fury exceeded all bounds, and he scrambled on to the bank and wrathfully demanded payment from everyone standing nearby for repairs to his net. In the ensuing clamour, it did not seem appropriate to suggest that since our mermaid appeared to be a particularly passionate one, we should go and find Mr. King so that he could stroke the ropes and pacify her the next time she was netted. The argument proceeded and everyone seemed to forget the manatee except Jack, who wandered off along the bank, tracing her course by swirls in the water.

At last the noise subsided. Jack called to Narian and pointed to where he had last seen the manatee.

Narian walked over, grumbling loudly, with a long rope in his hand.

"Dose mad men," he said contemptuously. "Dey bus' my net an he wu'th hundred dollar. *Dis* time I goin' in de water an' tie rope roun' her tail so she *cain't* escape."

He jumped into the lake again and waded to and fro, feeling for the manatee with his feet. At last he found her lying sluggishly on the bottom, and with the rope in his hands he bent down until his chin was just above the surface. He remained in this position for a few minutes as he groped in the water. Then he straightened and began to say something when the rope whipped tight in his hands, and pulled him flat on his face. He struggled to his feet, spat out the muddy water and happily brandished the end of the rope.

"I still got she," he called.

The manatee, having passively allowed the rope to be tied round her tail, now realized that she was in danger of being caught, and she reared to the surface, splashed and tried to bolt. This time Narian was ready for her and skilfully he managed to lead her towards the bank. His chastened assistants once more encircled the manatee with the net and Narian scrambled up onto the bank with the rope still in his hand. The men on the net pulled, Narian heaved, and slowly, tail first, the mermaid was hauled ashore.

On land she was not a pretty sight. Her head was little more than a blunt stump, garnished with an extensive but sparse moustache on her huge blubbery upper-lip. Her minute eyes were buried deep in the flesh of her cheek and would have been almost undetectable if they had not been suppurating slightly. Apart from her prominent nostrils, therefore, she possessed no feature which could give her any facial expression whatsoever. From her nose to the end of her great spatulate tail she was just over seven feet long. She had two paddle-shaped front flippers, but no rear limbs, and where she kept her bones was a mystery for, robbed of the support of the water, her great body slumped like a sack of wet sand.

She seemed entirely indifferent to our exploratory prods, and allowed herself to be turned over without so much as a wriggle of protest. As she lay motionless on her back, her flippers fallen outwards, I became worried that she had been injured during her capture, and I asked Narian if she was all right. He laughed. "Dis t'ing *cain't* die," he said, and splashed some water on her, whereupon she arched her body, slapped her tail on the ground and then returned to immobility.

The problem of getting her back to Georgetown was solved for us by the Town Council of New Amsterdam, who lent us the municipal water-lorry. We tied rope slings round her tail and beneath her flippers. Narian and his three assistants hoisted her from the ground and staggered across the meadow to where the lorry was parked.

Sagging between the slings, her flippers hanging down limply, and dribbling slightly from beneath her vast moustache, she hardly looked alluring. "If any sailor ever mistook *her* for a mermaid," Charles said, "I reckon he must have been at sea for a very long time."

CHAPTER
THIRTEEN

Return

Our expedition had come to an end. Jack and Tim were to bring the animals back to London by sea, but Charles and I had to return immediately by air to begin work on the film. Before we left Jack gave us a large square parcel. "Inside this," he said, "there are a few nice spiders, scorpions and one or two snakes. They are all in sealed tins with tiny air holes so there's no possibility of them escaping, but try and keep them with you in the cabin so that they don't catch cold. And will you also take this young coatimundi kitten?" he added, passing me a delightful little furry creature with bright brown eyes, a long ringed tail, and a pointed inquisitive snout. "He's still on a milk diet, so you will have to feed him from the bottle every three or four hours on your way back."

Charles and I climbed into the plane with the parcel and the coatimundi in a little travelling basket. The kitten was the object of a great deal of interest. As we flew over the islands of the Caribbean, a lady came to fondle him. She asked what sort of an animal he was, and how we came by him, and gradually we had to explain that we had been on an animal-collecting expedition. She looked at the box by my feet.

"I suppose," she said with a smile, "that that is full of snakes and other creepy-crawlies."

"As a matter of fact," I said in sepulchral tones, "*it is*," and we all laughed uproariously at such an absurd suggestion.

The coatimundi behaved very well for the first part of the journey, but as we began flying north towards Europe he refused his milk. Fearing that he might catch cold, I tucked him inside my shirt, where he nuzzled beneath my arm and slept peacefully. I tried to persuade him to feed again in Lisbon, and once more at Zürich, but though we heated the milk and even tempted him with mashed bananas and cream in a saucer, he still declined to feed. We arrived in Amsterdam at one o'clock in the morning. The London plane left at six. Charles and I settled down to wait on the long leather couches of the airport foyer. Our little kitten had not fed now for thirty-six hours and we were becoming very anxious about him. We searched our memories trying to recall what is the favourite food of a coatimundi, but we could only remember that they were described in the natural history books as being "omnivorous".

Charles had a brainwave. "What about some worms?" he said. "He might be tempted if they were nice and wriggly." I agreed, but neither of us was clear as to where we could get any worms at four o'clock in the morning in Amsterdam. Then it occurred to us that the Dutch, proud of their flowers, had surrounded the airfield with beautiful beds of plants which were now in full bloom. Leaving the kitten with Charles, I walked out on to the airfield, and in the glare of the floodlights

I surreptitiously waded into the flower-beds. Airport officials walked within a few feet of me as I dug in the soft earth with my fingers, but no one took the slightest notice and after five minutes I had over a dozen pink, wriggling worms. I took them back in triumph and to our delight the little coatimundi ate them greedily. When he had finished, he licked his lips and plainly asked for more. We made four more trips to the tulip bed before he was satisfied. Six hours later we handed him over, kicking lustily, to the London Zoo.

Back in Georgetown a great amount of work still remained to be done to get the animals ready for the long voyage home. The last few weeks of our trip had been clouded by Jack's increasing ill health. Slowly it became apparent that he had contracted an extremely serious paralysing illness, and a few days after we left him doctors in Georgetown recommended that he should be flown home as soon as possible to see a specialist in London. John Yelland, the Curator of Birds in the Zoo, flew out to Georgetown to take Jack's place and help Tim Vinall bring the collection to London by sea.

This was an arduous and complicated task: to ensure that the manatee had a comfortable trip, they arranged for a special canvas swimming bath to be erected on one of the decks of the ship; to cater for the enormous appetites of the animals they took on board a stock of provisions which included 3,000 lbs of lettuces, 100 lbs of cabbages, 400 lbs of bananas, 160 lbs of green grass and 48 pineapples; and to keep the collection clean and well fed on the nineteen-day voyage, Tim and John had to work unceasingly from dawn to dusk.

It was some weeks before I was able to go to the Zoo to see the animals again. I found the manatee swimming lazily to and fro in a crystal clear pool that had been specially built for her in the Aquarium. She was now so tame that when I leaned over and dabbled a cabbage leaf in the water, she swam to the side and took it from my hand. The little parrot that we had been given on the Kukui was now fully fledged and almost unrecognizable, but I convinced myself that he knew me, for when I talked to him he jerked his head up and down exactly as he had done when I had been feeding him chewed cassava bread from my mouth months before. The humming birds looked magnificent, darting and hovering among tropical plants in a specially heated house. Percy, the porcupine, I discovered curled up asleep in the angle of a branch, still with his unmistakable sour expression on his face. Chiquita, however, I was unable to recognize as she played on ropes and swings with several other capuchin monkeys.

When I found the capybara they were just about to leave for a large paddock in Whipsnade, the Zoo's country estate; they whistled and giggled and sucked my fingers as enthusiastically as they had done on the Barima. The anteaters still flourished on their diet of raw minced meat and milk, and in the Insect House I discovered that the spider we had caught at Arakaka had given birth a few days after it arrived to several hundred tiny young which were now fast growing up.

It took me some time to find Houdini, the animal that

had caused me personally more trouble than any other. When I at last discovered him he had his head down noisily champing and guzzling in a large dish of swill. I leaned over the wall of his paddock and called him several times. He ignored me completely.

INDEX OF PRINCIPAL ANIMALS